Y0-CBP-598

SuperSTAR Customer Service

It's all about C.A.R.E.

Rick Conlow
Doug Watsabaugh

A Crisp Fifty-Minute™ Series Book

AXZO  PRESS

SuperSTAR Customer Service

It's all about C.A.R.E.

Rick Conlow
Doug Watsabaugh

CREDITS:

President, Axzo Press:	**Jon Winder**
Vice President, Product Development:	**Charles G. Blum**
Vice President, Operations:	**Josh Pincus**
Director, Publishing Systems Development:	**Dan Quackenbush**
Copy Editor:	**Ken Maher**

COPYRIGHT © 2009 Axzo Press. All Rights Reserved.

No part of this work may be reproduced, transcribed, or used in any form or by any means—graphic, electronic, or mechanical, including photocopying, recording, taping, Web distribution, or information storage and retrieval systems—without the prior written permission of the publisher.

For more information, go to **www.CrispSeries.com**

Trademarks

Crisp Fifty-Minute Series is a trademark of Axzo Press.

Some of the product names and company names used in this book have been used for identification purposes only and may be trademarks or registered trademarks of their respective manufacturers and sellers.

Disclaimer

We reserve the right to revise this publication and make changes from time to time in its content without notice.

ISBN 10: 1-4260-1845-2
ISBN 13: 978-1-4260-1845-9
Printed in the United States of America
1 2 3 4 5 6 7 8 9 10 12 11 10 09

Table of Contents

About the Authors 1

About the Crisp 50-Minute Series 5

A Note to Instructors 6

Part 1: The Customer Service Challenge!   **7**

What Customer Service?..9

The Search for Superior Customer Service 10

SuperSTAR Customer Service..14

Summary 22

Part 2: Mental Psyche   **23**

Moment of Magic I: Mental Psyche 25

Summary 36

Part 3: The Greeting   **37**

Moment of Magic II: The Greeting..39

Summary 47

Part 4: Meeting the Need   **49**

Moment of Magic III: Meeting the Need..51

Summary 63

Part 5: Follow-Through   **65**

Moment of Magic IV: Follow-through 67

Summary 77

Part 6: Handling Problems   **79**

Moments of Magic V: Handling Problems 81

Summary 92

Appendix   **93**

SuperSTAR Customer Service..95

ii

About the Authors

Rick Conlow

A quick glance at his professional resume leaves you with the strong impression that effort and optimism are a winning combination. Case in point: With Rick by their side, clients have achieved double- and triple-digit improvement in their sales performance, quality, customer loyalty and service results over the past 20-plus years and earned more than 30 quality and service awards.

In a day and age when optimism and going the extra mile can sound trite, Rick has made them a differentiator. His clients include organizations that are leaders in their industries, as well as others that are less well-known. Regardless, their goals are his goals.

Rick's life view and extensive background in sales and leadership – as a general manager, vice president, training director, program director, national sales trainer, and consultant – are the foundation of his coaching, training and consulting services. Participants in Rick's experiential, "live action" programs walk away with ah-has, inspiration, and skills they can immediately put to use.

These programs include "BEST Selling!"; "Moments of Magic!"; "Excellence in Management!"; "SuperSTAR Service and Selling!"; "The Greatest Secrets of all Time!"; and "Good Boss/Bad Boss – Which One Are You?"

Rick has also authored Excellence in Management, Excellence in Supervision, Returning to Learning, and Moments of Magic.

When he's not engaging an audience or engrossed in a coaching discussion, this proud husband and father is most likely astride a weight bench or motorcycle, taking on the back roads and highways of Minnesota.

Doug Watsabaugh

Doug values being a "regular person," with his feet on the ground and head in the realities of the daily challenges his client's face. It's his heart for and experience in helping clients deal with difficult situations that distinguish him from other sales performance and leadership development consultants.

His knowledge of experiential learning and his skill at designing change processes and learning events have enabled him to measurably improve the lives of thousands of individuals and hundreds of organizations in a wide variety of industries – financial services, manufacturing, medical devices, consumer goods, and technology, to name a few.

Before starting his own business, Doug served as the director of operations for a national training institute and manager of organizational development for a major chemical company and was responsible for worldwide training and organizational development for the world's third largest toy company.

He was also a partner in Performance & Human Development LLC, a California company that published high-involvement experiential activities, surveys and instruments, interactive training modules, papers, and multimedia presentations.

Doug has co-authored two books with John E. Jones, Ph.D., and William L. Bearley, Ed. D.: *The New Fieldbook for Trainers*, published by HRD Press and Lakewood Publishing, and *The OUS Quality Item Pool*, about organizational survey items that measure Baldrige criteria.

He is a member of the American Society for Training and Development (ASTD), the Minnesota Quality Council, and The National Organization Development Network.

Doug's father taught him the value of hard work, and it paid dividends: He funded his college education playing guitar and singing with a rock 'n' roll band, experiencing a close call with fame when he played bass in concert with Chuck Berry. Not bad for a guy who admits to being "a bit shy."

While Doug's guitar remains a source of enjoyment, it pales in comparison to his number one joy and priority – his family.

WCW Partners

WCW Partners is a performance improvement company with more than 20 years of experience helping companies, governmental agencies, and nonprofit organizations worldwide revitalize their results and achieve record-breaking performance.

We are experts in sales performance, organizational development, leadership development, marketing, and communications – and we don't mind telling you that we're different from most consulting firms you find in the marketplace.

For one thing, it's our approach – when you hire us, you get us. But just as important, we're people who've had to wrestle with the same issues you have – how to strengthen sales, boost productivity, improve quality, increase employee satisfaction, build a team, or retain and attract new customers. To us, "We develop the capability in you" is more than a catchy phrase. It's our promise.

Our clients include 3M, American Express, American Medical Systems, Amgen Inc., Accenture, AmeriPride Services, Andersen Windows, Avanade, Beltone, Canadian Linen and Uniform Service, Carew International, Case Corporation, Citigroup, Coca-Cola, Costco, Covance, Deknatel, Eaton Corporation, Electrochemicals Inc., Entergy, Esoterix, General Mills, GN Resound, Grant Thornton, Hasbro Inc., Honeywell, Interton, Kenner Products, Marketlink, Kemps-Marigold, Meijer Corporation, National Computer Systems, Parker Brothers, Toro, Productive Workplace Systems, Red Wing Shoes, Rite Aid, Rollerblade, Ryan Companies, Travelers Insurance, Thrivent, Tonka Corporation, and a number of nonprofit and educational institutions.

To learn how you can do amazing things, visit us online at WCWPartners.com or contact Doug or Rick toll free at 1-888-313-0514.

Learning Objectives

Complete this book, and you'll know how to:

1) Discuss the elements of SuperSTAR Customer Service – including Moments of Truth, Misery, Mediocrity, and Magic – and learn to CARE for customers.

2) Apply Moment of Magic I: Mental Psyche.

3) Apply Moment of Magic II: The Greeting.

4) Apply Moment of Magic III: Meeting the Need.

5) Apply Moment of Magic IV: Follow-through.

6) Apply Moment of Magic V Handling Problems.

Workplace and Management Competencies mapping

For over 30 years, business and industry has utilized competency models to select employees. The trend to use competency-based approaches in education and training, assessment, and development of workers has experienced a more recent emergence within the Employment and Training Administration (ETA), a division of the United States Department of Labor.

The ETA's General Competency Model Framework spans a wide array of competencies from the more basic competencies, such as reading and writing, to more advanced occupation-specific competencies. The Crisp Series finds its home in what the ETA refers to as the Workplace Competencies and the Management Competencies.

SuperSTAR Customer Service covers information vital to mastering the following competencies:

Workplace Competencies:

▶ Adaptability & Flexibility

▶ Customer Focus

For a comprehensive mapping of Crisp Series titles to the Workplace and Management competencies, visit www.CrispSeries.com.

About the Crisp 50-Minute Series

The Crisp 50-Minute Series is designed to cover critical business and professional development topics in the shortest possible time. Our easy-to-read, easy-to-understand format can be used for self-study or for classroom training. With a wealth of hands-on exercises, the 50-Minute books keep you engaged and help you retain critical skills.

What You Need to Know

We designed the Crisp 50-Minute Series to be as self-explanatory as possible. But there are a few things you should know before you begin the book.

Exercises

Exercises look like this:

EXERCISE TITLE

Questions and other information are here.

Keep a pencil handy. Any time you see an exercise, you should try to complete it. If the exercise has specific answers, an answer key is provided in the appendix. (Some exercises ask you to think about your own opinions or situation; these types of exercises do not have answer keys.)

Forms

A heading like this means that the rest of the page is a form:

FORMHEAD

Forms are meant to be reusable. You might want to make a photocopy of a form before you fill it out, so that you can use it again later.

A Note to Instructors

We've tried to make the Crisp 50-Minute Series books as useful as possible as classroom training manuals. Here are some of the features we provide for instructors:

- ▶ PowerPoint presentations
- ▶ Answer keys
- ▶ Assessments
- ▶ Customization

PowerPoint Presentations

You can download a PowerPoint presentation for this book from our Web site at www.CrispSeries.com.

Answer keys

If an exercise has specific answers, an answer key will be provided in the appendix. (Some exercises ask you to think about your own opinions or situation; these types of exercises will not have answer keys.)

Assessments

For each 50-Minute Series book, we have developed a 35- to 50-item assessment. The assessment for this book is available at www.CrispSeries.com. *Assessments should not be used in any employee-selection process.*

Customization

Crisp books can be quickly and easily customized to meet your needs—from adding your logo to developing proprietary content. Crisp books are available in print and electronic form. For more information on customization, see www.CrispSeries.com.

The Customer
Service Challenge!

> *'I must do something'* always solves more problems than *'Something must be done.'"*

–Anonymous

In this part:

▶ What Customer Service?

▶ The Search for Superior Customer Service

▶ SuperSTAR Customer Service

What Customer Service?

An intelligent and caring woman named Pam hustled to her bank to deposit her paycheck thinking that she'd beat the noontime rush. Standing in line at the bank, Pam waited quite a while for a teller who finally shouted, "Next!" with all the empathy of a prison guard. She puzzled over the teller's behavior.

Later that day, as Pam waited at the airport for a flight, a monotone voice over the intercom announced that her plane was delayed… again. When she finally boarded, she found the plane crowded with passengers who'd left their manners in the terminal. Worse, she couldn't find room in the overhead bin for her bag. A preoccupied flight attendant wasn't much help. "Try the back of the plane," he barked. Why couldn't the crew member apologize for the delay, Pam wondered, or at least help her store her belongings?

By the time Pam arrived at her hotel, it was late. When she checked in, she asked for an important package that she'd forwarded, but it was nowhere to be found. The exhausted clerk told her she'd have to wait until morning, because "no one knows anything on the night shift." When Pam objected, the clerk responded, "I don't know anything, lady! Come back in the morning!" At this point, it was clear that the bag of stale pretzels she'd received on the plane wouldn't sustain her until morning. So Pam dialed room service, but no one answered the phone.

She found a nearby restaurant and wearily dropped into the first booth. The waitress took her order and delivered it. The service was… mechanical, she thought, just average. It wasn't horrible like her earlier encounters at the bank, airline, and hotel, but it wasn't good, either.

Pam walked back to her hotel, becoming more and more distressed about the day's events. She suddenly realized that her difficult day with customer service people really wasn't that remarkable. She received this level of service on most trips. So many people lack that "something extra" when serving customers, she thought. It seems that customers like me have become so used to poor service, we've become indifferent. Our expectations are really low. Why can't service be better?

Can you relate to Pam's experience? Why do many people in service positions seem uncaring and display poor attitudes? Why don't they treat customers with more courtesy, respect, and dignity? Excellent customer service seems to be the exception these days. Why do we allow this? We have many choices for most things we buy. Are you tired of poor service? How do you feel as a customer in those situations? Why is there a lack of exceptional customer service in so many businesses?

All jobs require customer service. How well do you provide service to others? You can provide SuperSTAR Customer Service and deliver Moments of Magic to the customers you have one at a time. That's what this book is all about. You'll learn about and work with the strategies of the very best in customer service. These SuperSTARs surpass the norm and give extraordinary customer service on a consistent basis. You can, too! We wish you and your customers the best of success.

The Search for Superior Customer Service

Pam's experience drove her to search for exceptional customer service by becoming an aware customer. She paid more attention to how people delivered service. She found research from a variety of sources, such as the Technical Assistance Research Project, the US Office of Consumer Affairs, Product Marketing and Profit Impact Marketing Strategy. Her research showed that companies with the best service:

▶ Charge more for their product.

▶ Enjoy stronger customer retention.

▶ Gain market share.

▶ Earn more profit.

▶ Offer greater job security and opportunities to their employees.

She began to evaluate their approaches. She created a three-point scale by which to rate customer service people and companies: Poor, Average, or Excellent.

"I feel strangely drawn to this company."

Poor Service

"Poor" means a lack of concern or care. Unfortunately, some people might be better suited for jobs in the back room or, perhaps, might benefit from extensive training. This group includes the waitress who walked up to a couple in her section, stuck out a hip, and said, "Hurry up and order. I'm on break in a few minutes!" It includes traders who sold worthless derivatives to their clients. Did they want to satisfy their customers?

Average Service

Pam determined that "average" service was only mediocre. She learned of a retailer that had been #1 for years. If people needed clothes, tools, appliances or electronics, they patronized this company. However, the company became so large that it lost focus and seemed to lose sight of customers' changing needs. Being average means you don't get better, and if there are problems, you point your finger in another direction. Average customer service people do just enough to get by. Yet, companies in this category can't say they're average. Could you imagine a company with the slogan, "We are no worse than anyone else"? Wow! Now that's a phrase to motivate employees and customers alike. Instead, these companies claim to have good service. In reality they do little to distinguish themselves.

Excellent Service

"Excellent" customer service people really care, project great attitudes, and extend themselves to make customers feel special. The people or companies who fall into this category are better, faster, and different. These attributes help employees to be promoted and rise to the top in their companies. The best companies in any industry tend to have the best customer service.

Excellent service is the waitress who smiles but also pays attention to you and has a sense of humor. It's the airline attendant who greets you when you get on the plane and creates a fun atmosphere for the trip. It's the friendly employees in a grocery store who go out of their way to help you. It's the plumber who explains what he did and calls back later to see if everything is still okay. And it's the pharmacist who is courteous and helpful and takes time for your questions. Excellent performers routinely go the extra mile. These people become the superstars.

Pam traveled frequently and began to take note of the level of service provided by organizations she frequented: clothing stores, computer outlets, car dealers, restaurants, hotels, banks, airlines, printing companies, catalog distributors, specialty shops, car rental agencies, art galleries, and furniture stores. In her travels, she visited both national manufacturing headquarters and local job shops.

Pam spoke with many customer service people. She was committed to improving her own results. Her search led her to the leading authorities on customer service: authors, consultants, educators, quality gurus, and speakers. She read books and attended seminars. She learned the lingo and knew the right phrases.

She began to understand the full range and level of customer service delivered by individuals and their organizations. She wasn't impressed. With all the attention customer service and quality have received, it still appears that many employees don't know how to take care of customers. She was perplexed as to why so little has changed over the last few years—especially since research says customer service and loyalty are crucial to the long-term success of any organization, and studies demonstrate the significance of great service to a company's profit and survival.

Pam also looked for customer service people and companies who care and deliver excellent service. She wanted to do more than meet customers' expectations. She wanted to exceed them.

She learned to identify poor customer service people—an easy task given there are so many of them. Unfortunately, they can wreak havoc with a customer in a hurry. Most poor service people or organizations are self-centered or looking for a fast buck and possess one or more easy-to-recognize characteristics.

She knew that some poor performers' companies supported their actions in some strange way. Why? She didn't understand, because she knew that poor customer service drives customers away.

TOP 10 POOR SERVICE BEHAVIORS: CHECKLIST

Check the poor service behaviors you have seen as a customer.

- ☐ Don't care
- ☐ Discourtesy and lack for friendliness
- ☐ Rudeness
- ☐ Lack of knowledge of product or service
- ☐ Lack of attentiveness or responsiveness to problems
- ☐ Making customers wait too long

- ☐ Poor listening skills
- ☐ Lack of follow-through
- ☐ Lack of empathy
- ☐ Dishonesty

Pam noticed that the vast majority of customer service people fall into the "average" category. Again, the job titles of average customer service people vary from the owner to the store greeter. She marveled that nearly all of them think they deliver exceptional service. While many do care and try hard, their efforts can fall short. Something is missing. Sometimes they even drop from average to poor due to their mood. These employees and their organizations do little to distinguish themselves. She heard these excuses:

- ▶ I'm doing the best I can.

- ▶ I'm really trying hard.

- ▶ I'm not getting enough help from others. If only they would do their jobs.

- ▶ My manager doesn't care.

- ▶ I can only do so much.

- ▶ The customers are unreasonable and don't understand.

Unfortunately, Pam discovered that supervisors and companies usually accept their excuses. After all, they do provide "good" service. As a customer, she'd experienced the truth—they were mediocre at best. Their service mantra really was, "We are no worse than anyone else."

Pam was disappointed to find so few people who deliver excellent service. None of them think they have any secrets to share. And, they have a hard time explaining how they do it. But when they served her, she certainly experienced a difference. Excellent customer service people resemble the others in some ways. For example, they work in the same organizations and jobs as less-effective service people. However, they're more upbeat, knowledgeable, and helpful. And their results are superior. They delight their customers with excellence when others don't. If only more people and organizations knew how they do it, she thought. She was eager to find out what makes these rare individuals so successful.

Pam heard fabulous stories about an excellent service person in a nearby town whose customers flocked to him for assistance. His successes were legendary. She wondered if the stories were really true and, if so, whether he would talk to her and share his "magic." Curious, she decided to see for herself, so she called the car dealership where he worked as a service advisor. He promptly answered the phone, "Good afternoon. This is Joe in service. How may I help you?"

Pam explained who she was and what she wanted. Joe listened, praised her enthusiasm and follow-through, and told her he couldn't talk in detail now because he was on "customer time." He said after work would be fine. Then, he asked, "By the way, Pam, does your car need an oil change?"

Surprised by the question, Pam said "yes" and made an appointment for the early part of the next week. She was intrigued by her contact with Joe and looked forward to meeting him.

SuperSTAR Customer Service

The night before her appointment, she found a message from Joe on her answering machine, reminding her about her oil change appointment. Pam appreciated the gesture, reminded of the times she'd been so wrapped up in her work that she'd missed appointments.

When she arrived at the dealership the next day and entered the service area, she noticed Joe. He was working with two other customers, but glanced up at her, waved slightly and smiled. Within a few minutes, he finished with the others and greeted her politely. "Welcome to Cartown. I'm Joe, at your service," he said. Then he shook her hand, asked a few questions about her car and explained how the oil change process, which included a safety check, would work. Afterward, he escorted her to the customer lounge.

Before he left, he asked, "Pam, why don't we discuss your questions about customer satisfaction after I finish work? I'm off customer time at 6:30 p.m." Pam agreed. He pointed out the coffee machine and work area in the lounge if she needed it and promised to return in 30 minutes.

He returned within the specified time with a list of recommended maintenance and asked if she wanted it handled now or if she wanted to schedule an appointment. Pam made an appointment for two weeks out. Joe directed Pam to the cashier, cheerfully thanked her for the business, and said he looked forward to talking with her later that day. In a moment, he'd greeted another customer with a welcome and a smile.

Pam left the dealership feeling pleased with the consideration she'd received. She noticed the outside of her car was washed and the inside vacuumed. Joe left a thank you note on her passenger seat with his business card inside and attached a yellow ribbon to the steering wheel (as a reminder to drive safely). She understood why Joe was so highly regarded. He really seemed to care.

That evening, Pam and Joe met for coffee. She told him her story, and Joe listened actively. She explained her expansive search for excellent customer service and told him about her customer service ratings—poor, average and excellent. Finally, Joe spoke. "Pam, there aren't any secrets to customer service." As she began to object, he quickly added, "But there are five crucial 'Moments of Truth.'"

"A Moment of Truth is anything you do that affects a customer's perception of you and your organization. These could include how you spell a customer's name, your level of courtesy, your handling of a question, demonstrating or finding a product, listening, offering options, and whether or not you say 'thank you' at the end of a transaction. These Moments of Truth add up and create dissatisfied or happy customers. When you self-manage these Moments of Truth effectively, you create Moments of Magic for your customers. Your customers recognize how well you treat them and how good your service is. I call it 'SuperSTAR Customer Service.' That's where you exceed the customers' expectations and, in nearly every case, satisfy customers so they want to come back."

"Like you did with my oil change," Pam offered.

"Well, yes, and thank you," said Joe. "Now if you do less than the customer expects, it's what you call poor service. You produce what I call 'Moments of Misery' and an unhappy customer. In today's competitive business arena, SuperSTAR Customer Service equals excellence. Anything less is unacceptable," he said.

Moment of Truth: *Anything you do that directly affects the customer's perception of you or your organization.*

Moment of Misery: *When you do less than the customer expects.*

Moment of Mediocrity: *When you only meet the customer's expectations.*

Moment of Magic: *When you exceed the customer's expectations.*

"Let me show you what I mean about Moments of Truth. Then he drew a diagram on a sheet of paper. He explained each step of the diagram as he wrote.

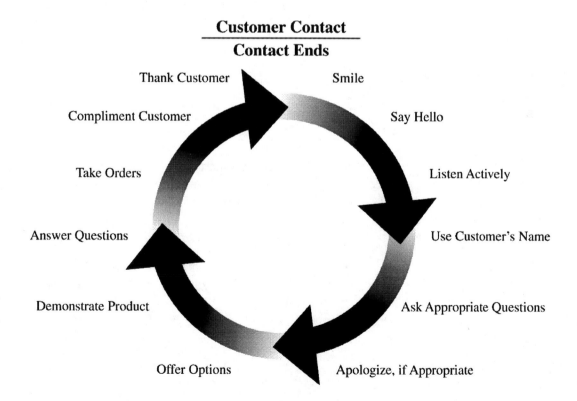

Customer Contact

Contact Ends

Thank Customer — Smile — Say Hello — Listen Actively — Use Customer's Name — Ask Appropriate Questions — Apologize, if Appropriate — Offer Options — Demonstrate Product — Answer Questions — Take Orders — Compliment Customer

"As you can see, there are twelve basic Moments of Truth here," Joe explained. "Depending on the situation, there could be more or less. It takes one moment of magic to overcome twenty minutes of misery. Many Moments of Truth are the small quick things we do unconsciously. Each Moment of Truth matters. This is just an example. Poor service people skip some or manage them poorly. They usually produce Moments of Misery for customers. Mediocre or good customer service people attempt most of the important Moments of Truth, but they usually produce average, more-of-the-same, easy-to-forget service. Excellence comes from SuperSTARs. Customers walk away impressed, feeling good and ready to tell everyone they know. The SuperSTARs really understand customer C-A-R-E (He spelled the word)."

"What do you mean C-A-R-E?" Pam asked, excitedly.

"Creating Moments of Magic for customers means you CARE. While anyone can do it, she must believe in and act on it regardless of the situation," said Joe.

Joe wrote CARE on a piece of paper:

C ustomers (or co-workers)

A re

R eally

E everything

"Without loyal customers, a business or organization doesn't exist. People like us have no jobs. The purpose of a business is to create the highest level of customer satisfaction and loyalty. Fantastic service requires teamwork, too, so SuperSTAR customer service people treat their internal customers—their co-workers—to Moments of Magic as well. When Moments of Truth are managed consistently, word travels fast and far. Business profits and success follow. This result has been well researched and documented.

"Employees are frequently self-centered in their approach to customers, including internal customers. They are too concerned about their personal needs or problems really to care about customer needs or wants. Problems, such as being tired, angry with their spouse, worried about finances, being the victim of rude treatment, or feeling unappreciated by their company can sidetrack customer focus," he added.

"While these are just examples and could be difficult personal situations, none of these scenarios warrants treating customers poorly. If you CARE, you rise above personal issues, focus on others and provide excellent service by self-managing five key Moments of Magic. I'll briefly discuss these with you, then refer you to two other people who can help you in your search. Afterwards, we can talk again. Sound okay?" Joe asked.

"Great," Pam agreed.

"Many years ago, motivator and businessman Bob Conklin taught me that, if you give other people what they want, you'll get what you want. Providing SuperSTAR Customer Service means you take this axiom one step further. My goal is to treat customers much better than they expect. I've found it comes back tenfold over time."

"I understand," said Pam, "but it's difficult to do what you describe if your company doesn't care or you aren't feeling up to the task. Then what?"

"Unfortunately," said Joe, "some companies don't help much. Even with all the emphasis on quality and service, too many companies aren't walking the talk. Some might go out of business if they don't become more customer-focused. But a company's lack of commitment is no excuse for a true SuperSTAR customer service person. In spite of organizational obstacles or personal problems, SuperSTARs understand that it takes only a few moments to satisfy a customer and that each customer counts. SuperSTARs are determined to make a positive difference with each customer contact, one person at a time. So, they take ownership and individual responsibility to do the right things for customers."

"Why don't all customer service people do this?" questioned Pam.

"It usually comes down to two things: attitude and skill," responded Joe. "Without both, you don't get the necessary result." He drew a chart on another sheet of paper to explain the four quadrants in his customer service matrix.

"Attitude means being self-centered or other-centered." If you're self-centered, you focus on your problems. If you're other-centered, you focus on the customer's needs. Skill involves low or high ability in communicating and working with people. Both skill and attitude can be learned.

		Skill	
		Low	High
Will	High	I. Learners: Moments of Mediocrity	II. SuperSTAR Customer Service: Moments of Magic
	Low	III. Poor Service Providers: Moments of Misery	IV. Average Service Providers: Moments of Mediocrity

"People in Quadrants I and IV create mediocre Moments of Truth for customers. They give average service, at best. Quadrant I service people have the potential to deliver SuperSTAR Customer Service. They care, but they need training support and experience to develop their communication and customer service skills. They're the learners.

"Those in Quadrant IV could deliver SuperSTAR Customer Service, but they don't care and aren't committed enough. They don't understand or use the first Moment of Magic, so daily problems or personal issues become formidable barriers to them. They have the skill but are unable to deliver consistently because of their self-centered attitudes. They're average customer service people. They aren't willing to take additional steps to provide consistently the help that generates high customer satisfaction and loyalty.

"People in Quadrant III are poor service people. They don't enjoy helping others. Even if they have the skill, they don't use it. The results are Moments of Misery.

"The best service people are in Quadrant II. They have the skill and the will to help others. They deliver SuperSTAR Customer Service. Customers know and appreciate it. They return to these individuals who CARE and back it up with action."

"Well, what are these Moments of Magic you've referred to?" asked Pam.

Joe handed Pam a sheet of paper and rattled off five: Mental Psyche, Greeting, Meeting the Need, Follow-through, and Handling Problems.

Mental
Psyche

Follow-through

Greeting

C.A.R.E.

Handling
Problems

Meeting
Needs

The SuperSTAR Customer Service Model

SuperSTAR Customer Service

The goal is to treat customers much better than they expect by self-managing five moments of magic.

Anxious to get home to see his children before their bedtime, Joe wouldn't elaborate. But he did give Pam the names of two other people. "They know all about Moments of Magic and will give you more details. Then come back and see me again."

"I really have to go. I'll see you soon, though," he offered. "Good-bye."

"Good-bye and thanks!" Pam replied as she headed for the door. She drove home overwhelmed. Her meeting with Joe was more than she'd expected. Finally, she was learning the specifics of excellent service. According to Joe, it was the customer service person's responsibility. No excuses. In her mind, she reviewed what Joe had told her about Moments of Truth, Magic, and Misery, CARE service approaches, the Cycle of Service, and the Customer Service Matrix. She found she was anxious to meet the people to whom Joe had referred her.

SUPERSTAR APPLICATION: MOMENTS OF TRUTH

Describe two memorable service experiences, one poor and one excellent, where you were the customer. As you describe the two situations, identify what the customer service people did to make it poor or excellent.

Poor experience: _____

_____

Identify three to five Moments of Misery for your poor experience:

1. _____
2. _____
3. _____
4. _____
5. _____

Excellent experience: _____

_____

Identify three to five Moments of Magic for your excellent experience:

1. _____
2. _____
3. _____
4. _____
5. _____

SuperSTAR Application: Cycle of Service

Fill in the Cycle of Service Model below for your job. Be as specific as possible in listing the Moments of Truth. When you're finished, check the results with a co-worker, a customer, and your supervisor. Then take consistent action in your job. Remember to create Moments of Magic. Exceed the customer's expectations. That's what SuperSTARs do!

Cycle of Service

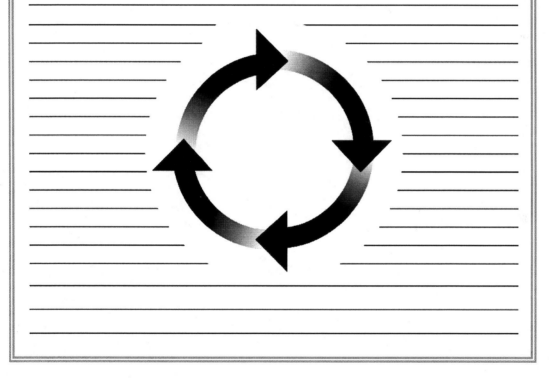

Summary

In this part, you learned to evaluate customer service as either **poor, average**, or **excellent**. You learned that customer service interactions can produce **Moments of Truth, Moments of Misery, Moments of Mediocrity**, or **Moments of Magic**. Next, you learned that **SuperSTAR Customer Service** exceeds customer expectations. Then you learned the **Cycle of Service**. You learned that you can create Moments of Magic when you **CARE**, and you learned the **CARE Customer Service Model**.

Mental Psyche

> **The first step to being a superstar in customer service has nothing to do with the customer. It has everything to do with you."**
>
> –Rick Conlow

In this part:

▶ Moment of Magic I: Mental Psyche

Moment of Magic I: Mental Psyche

The first person on Pam's list was Susan, an insurance representative. When Pam arrived at Susan's office, she found a woman with a telephone pressed against her ear surrounded by mounds of paper and files. Susan signaled her to sit down and, within a few moments, said hello.

"Welcome to Mid-County Insurance. I'm Susan. It's good to see you. Joe told me all about you. By the way, he took great care of your car, didn't he? He handles mine, and I never have to worry. So… he also told you about being a SuperSTAR customer service person?"

"Yes, he did, and I'm really curious," Pam replied. "Is there anything really special about it?"

"There sure is, and it all begins with Mental Psyche," said Susan. "It's the foundation for CARE behavior. It sets the tone. Without Mental Psyche, average is the best a service person can be. And as I'm sure Joe told you, average is nothing more than doing just enough to get by. It's vanilla customer service."

"Mental Psyche sounds like a motivational speech," said Pam. "How do you do it?"

"Have you ever encountered a crabby checkout person at a department store? Chances are the clerk knew the job well enough. He could run the cash register, right? And he probably knew the products in his area. Yet, he treated you poorly. Why?" asked Susan.

Pam thought for a while and then suggested that the person may have been tired, sick or was thinking about a personal problem.

Susan interjected, "How did that person make you feel?"

"I felt embarrassed," described Pam. "He was rude, and I got uneasy standing there. I even made an abrupt remark to him about waiting in line too long. Later, while driving home, I was angry at him, at the store, and at myself for letting him get away with that behavior. I avoid that store now."

"Exactly!" Susan jumped in. "Treat customers poorly, and they'll treat you poorly. Treat them well, and they return the favor. The first Moment of Magic is Mental Psyche. Even if a salesperson, a manager, or a customer service person is having a bad day, it's her job to serve the customer with CARE. She must learn how to set aside, forget, or work through all negative emotions or attitudes and serve the customer properly. Use the Mental Psyche process before serving customers – especially when you aren't well, feel depressed, or feel that others aren't supportive. Just take a few moments on a break or in between customers to prepare yourself mentally. The Mental Psyche approach helps you become other-centered. It also helps you to feel better about yourself and the job you're doing. People who feel good about themselves deliver CARE service, regardless of the situation or circumstances."

"How do you mean?" asked Pam.

People who feel good about themselves deliver SuperSTAR customer service, regardless of the situation or the circumstances."

"It begins by acknowledging how you're feeling," said Susan. "Have you ever noticed that, when one thing goes wrong, it's easy for something else to go wrong? If you let negative emotions overwhelm you, they tend to spill onto your customers. You can stop the overflow by reviewing how you feel. By taking a moment to consider how you're doing, you position yourself to respond with CARE."

"So how do you do this?" asked Pam.

"Start by saying or admitting to yourself that you're tired, upset, or cross. Then remind yourself that you like to be treated with CARE and that it's your job to treat customers the same way. Next, remind yourself of your No. 1 goal: To take care of customers and exceed expectations, because in the long run, your job depends on it. Customers have many choices today. Nearly any product or service can be purchased in a variety of ways or places."

"I don't know what's in it either, but
I know you shouldn't make it too hot or too cold."

"You know, you're right," Pam said. "There are any number of computer stores, car dealerships, restaurants, colleges, hotels, and airlines. All of them want my money. The customer's power is in her ability to choose."

"That's right," added Susan. "We can't let a bad day ruin customer relationships. So after you remind yourself of the customers' importance, visualize success. See yourself helping and satisfying both past and current customers. This also recognizes your own ability to do the job. It's self-appreciation. Verbalize or affirm that being a CARE service person is the right thing to do. Then, act and vitalize it by helping the next customer with a smile. It's hard to greet a customer positively with a frown, isn't it? All it takes is a few moments of mental review."

"Where did you learn this?" asked Pam.

"Joe taught me," said Susan. "He learned it from a luxury car salesman named Charlie. Charlie sold cars for 40 years and won numerous honors for sales and customer satisfaction. Joe asked him how, and Charlie replied, 'Mental Psyche.' Charlie said Mental Psyche gives you a positive ATTITUDE." Then Susan grabbed a pen and dashed out the following on a piece of paper.

Mental Psyche

Visualize—see it!

Verbalize—say it!

Vitalize—do it!

$$A + T + T + I + T + U + D + E$$

$$1 + 20 + 20 + 9 + 20 + 21 + 4 + 5 = 100\% \text{ commitment!}$$
(The numbers denote the letters' numerical place in the alphabet.)

"This all sounds wonderful," said Pam. "But it can be hard to do at times."

"You're right," Susan responded. "But what's the flip side? You're feeling bad or upset, you treat a customer badly, the customer treats you badly, your company loses a customer, and it happens all over again with the next customer. Now you feel even worse. It's a negative spiral. Mental Psyche is a way to break that spiral or prevent it from happening in the first place. Mental Psyche gives you the opportunity to give customers SuperSTAR Customer Service. Without Mental Psyche, it's tough to do, because problems or tedium can overwhelm us. So the first step to creating moments of magic has nothing to do with customers. It has everything to do with you! It's how you stay positive and focus on the customer in spite of the difficulties involved. For example, the best athletes in the world understand that their biggest challenge is mental rehearsal and preparation."

"Do you use Mental Psyche even when you're feeling okay?"

"Sure," replied Susan. "It makes you that much better. Mental Psyche takes only a few moments at the beginning of a day or during a day to keep you focused on the most important part of your job: the customer. Mental Psyche helps you learn to be positive and customer-focused, even when you don't feel like it. And, I think you'd agree with me, Pam, we all have our good days and bad, but does the customer really care or even need to know? Certainly not! The hard times are what separate the SuperSTARs from the rest. By the way, I have an appointment in 10 minutes, and I need to prepare. Why don't you do a quick summary of our discussion before we close our meeting?"

Mental Psyche: Review

"Let's see," started Pam. "Mental Psyche is self-managed preparation. It's what you do to focus on the customer regardless of circumstances. Begin your day with it or use it during the day, especially if you're busy or feeling upset. Don't take it out on customers. It's not their fault. Your job is to CARE for them. The first step to satisfying customers has nothing to do with them but is all about your attitude and approach to the job. There are six steps that take only a few moments mentally:

1. Acknowledge your feelings about the problem that distracts you.

2. Remind yourself how you want to be treated, then think of the customer.

3. Remember the importance of the customer.

4. Visualize yourself serving the customers well. See it!

5. Verbalize that you can do it, it's the right thing to do, and that you CARE. Say it!

6. Vitalize by serving the next customer with a smile. Do it!

"I guess, if you think the right things, you'll do the right things."

"That's pretty much it," said Susan. "Nice job. I think you're beginning to understand. Remember, though, it's only the start. The other Moments of Magic must follow, but without Mental Psyche, they seldom do." Susan said that she was running short on time, so they agreed to meet in a few days to discuss Moment of Magic II: Greeting.

"I look forward to it," Pam said.

As Pam sat at home that night reflecting, she made some notes. Mental Psyche is so simple, yet so powerful, she wrote. If you let your own concerns bother you, you're more likely to treat the customer poorly. Mental Psyche helps you do your best, even when you don't feel like it. It helps you stay other-centered and CARE about the customer, even when you're having a bad day. So the first step to taking care of a customer has less to do with the customer and more to do with yourself! Without the right attitude through Mental Psyche it's hard to do anything else right. She looked forward to talking with Susan again.

> *Mental Psyche is self-managed preparation. It helps you CARE about the customer in all circumstances.*"

Pam searched the Internet to see what she could learn about attitude and staying positive. She found the following material which supported what Joe described.

Emotional Resiliency and SuperSTAR Performance

Decades ago, Dr. Evan Kane felt doctors were losing too many patients in appendectomy surgery—many because of the effects of general anesthesia. He felt that local anesthesia would be better for the patient but, not surprisingly, no volunteers came forward to test his hypothesis. Until, that is, February 15, 1921. That's when he finally performed an appendectomy with local anesthesia -- on himself! In the process, he changed accepted medical practice.

HOW MANY DO YOU SEE?

To be your best, you often need to change too. Sometimes that change means operating on yourself! Begin analyzing your own situation simply by counting the number of times the letter "F" appears in the following sentence.

FEATURE FILMS ARE THE RE-

SULT OF YEARS OF SCIENTI-

FIC STUDY COMBINED WITH THE

FORMAL EXPERIENCE OF YEARS.

How many did you count? _____

How many did you get? Three? Five? There are a total of seven! If you missed some, why? Why would anyone miss an "F"—or two or three? This little exercise points out that what you're missing in terms of customer service performance improvement is most likely right in front of you. Sometimes the solutions to your challenges are there, but you just don't see them. Why? Because of entrenched habits, perceptions, and beliefs. When you try to improve, it may seem like trying to lose weight with fad diets or keeping New Year's resolutions. To begin, remember these important principles:

First, remember self-improvement is self-management. You can't change others or, sometimes, your situation, but you can change yourself. To manage yourself better to serve customers more effectively, you must be willing to change some habits to increase productivity.

Second, a foundation of self-management is responding to all events based on goals and priorities rather than reacting to spot urgencies, problems, or needs. So set clear goals in terms of what you want out of life. If you want to better your life, you have to learn to get beyond disappointments. Everyone has them. The key is how you respond to them. After being knocked down, how quickly do you get back up without resentment or blame for troubles? Write three to five goals in each area. Be specific, believe in the possibilities, and take action today. Clear goals give meaning to life and help you rise above circumstances. That's a key to SuperSTAR service as well.

MY GOALS

Personal Goals: Vitalize!	Career Goals: Vitalize!

Third, mind and body are intricately intertwined; to control what you do, better control what you think. Say positive affirmations, such as, "I can do this" or "I will succeed" or "I'm a successful and happy person" or "I'm persistent and determined to do all that I do with excellence." Do this instead of "I can't" or "I won't." In the blank space below, write a few positive affirmations of your own.

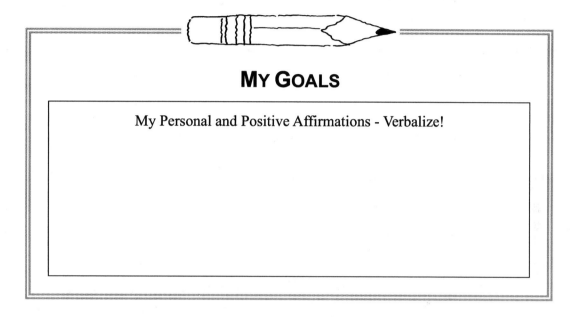

MY GOALS

My Personal and Positive Affirmations - Verbalize!

Fourth, visualize success and use all the moments of magic to help the next customer you see. Have a sense of urgency to succeed! In the space below describe the kind of success you want in your current job and career.

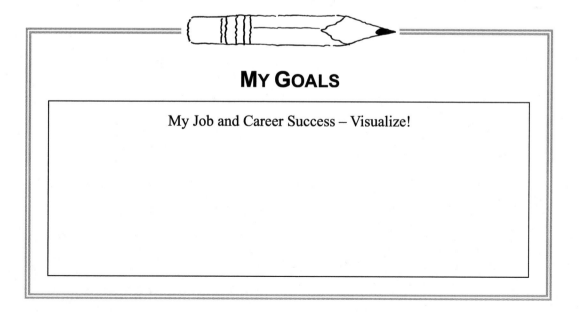

MY GOALS

My Job and Career Success – Visualize!

So what's the key to success? How do you break through? Dr. Charles Garfield of the Peak Performance Institute found that mental preparation helps individuals tap their personal best performances. Garfield experienced these techniques himself as a world- class weightlifter and researcher. Garfield explains, " In the process, the researchers discovered that mental training techniques not only combated negative reactions but also threw open the doors to hidden reserves of energy and endurance."

Dr. Denis Waitley identified similar peak performance strategies in his work with Olympic athletes and business people. These techniques relate to visualizing, verbalizing, and vitalizing.

Through practice, learn these techniques to become positive unconscious habits and the beginning of your SuperSTAR Customer Service. Be patient and, over time, you'll learn to do this well. Then you'll be able to use the other moments of magic most effectively.

Moment of Magic I: Mental Psyche

Purpose

Become a superstar by being prepared mentally to serve customers enthusiastically and positively every time every day. Take a few moments before each customer contact, especially when you feel bad. Make it an unconscious habit through practice.

Action Steps

1. Acknowledge how you're feeling.

2. Remind yourself how you would want to be treated as a customer—with CARE.

3. Remember how important customers are to your job. (Without them, there's no job.) Customer satisfaction is your No. 1 priority.

4. **Visualize** yourself helping and caring for each customer with excellence. Picture the customer really appreciating your effort. **See it!**

5. **Verbalize** that this is the right thing to do and that you do CARE. **Say it!**

6. **Vitalize** by helping the next customer with a smile! **Do it!**

These six points come from peak performance research to help people become top performers—superstars. Let's look at each of the action steps.

1. Acknowledge how you're feeling.

What do you notice about who's the focus in action step one? It's you, of course. To become customer-focused, you must first look inward. Think about how you're feeling and what you want. Be self=centered for a minute. How are you feeling? Frustrated? Tired? Overwhelmed? Excited? Optimistic? These feelings aren't good or bad—they're just feelings.

Shakespeare's Hamlet said, "To thine own self be true." It's human nature to do this sometimes. It's also honest to acknowledge that you're doing it. Quite frankly, superstars have more integrity than others. Why? They set big goals, and they think about how they can achieve them. They analyze their behavior and attitude. This mental time becomes their launching pad to do what they have to do to win, even if they don't feel like it at the moment. They remind themselves of their goals, personal commitment, and the payoff for acting with good intentions now. The key then becomes what you do with your feelings.

2. Remind yourself how you would want to be treated— with CARE.

This is a mental shift. Who do you begin to think about now? The customer-- this is critical to success. Regardless of how you're feeling you now, become other-centered, not self-centered. How can you deliver superstar service if you think only about yourself? You can't. (This is especially important if you're feeling negative or depressed about things.) Albert Schweitzer said, "I don't know what your destiny will be, but one thing I do know: the only ones among us who will be happy are those who have sought and learned how to serve." So, remind yourself of what customers want. According to research they want:

- ▶ Friendliness, kindness, and courtesy
- ▶ Knowledgeable and competent service
- ▶ Understanding and timely help with problems
- ▶ Follow through on commitments and promise
- ▶ Responsiveness with a willingness to serve

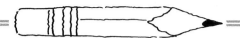

SuperSTAR Application 3: Mental Psyche

Most people find things in their jobs that frustrate or stress them. While these stressors can make it difficult to serve customers, the customer still deserves your best. Identify what frustrates or stresses you and how you can handle it. Then review Mental Psyche and commit the process to memory.

Frustrations/Stresses	How to Handle
1. Angry customers	Listen, and don't take it personally.
2.	
3.	
4.	
5.	
6.	
7.	
8.	
9.	
10.	

3. Remember how important customers are to your job.

Each employee must take total responsibility and accountability for customer service. Each day, customer service staff have thousands, if not millions, of moments of truth with customers. While you won't be able to deal with all of those, you can deal with the moments of truth for the customer in front of you. You can do it well and go the extra mile. Why? With hard work and determination, you can do just about anything. Plus, customer retention is the number one priority and the key to your success and job security.

4. Visualize yourself helping and caring for each customer. See it!

Top performers in sports always see a positive result before they take action. Visualization is often called the master skill of success. How do you do it? You take a few moments to think of how you want things to be. Picture it in your mind's eye as vividly as possible. Play a video in your mind of you succeeding and doing well. Create the feeling of success that will go with it. Do this as often as you can and, in time, your thoughts will help create the fact or a reality very close to it. Why visualize? It replaces worry and fear and helps you focus on what you can do and are capable of doing.

5. Verbalize that this is the right thing to do and that you do CARE. Say it!

Successful people use positive affirmations to help them succeed. First you see it, and then you say it. Obviously, you aren't going to walk down the street and say, "I am the best at customer service." People will stare. You can say it to yourself. Why? It replaces the doubt and negative thinking. Who controls your thoughts? You do; your thoughts come from your choices. Choose to think positively, and if you can't, then repeat affirmations to get your there.

6. Vitalize by helping the next customer with a smile! Do it now!

See it, say it, and do it now. You have to take action to take care of customers. That's what it's all about, and by following these steps, you'll do it with enthusiasm and excitement.

> *"The greatest discovery of our generation is that people can alter the outer aspects of their lives by changing the inner attitudes of their minds."*
>
> **–William James**

Summary

In this part, you learned that **Mental Psyche** is **Moment of Magic I**. You learned to **acknowledge** what you're feeling. Next, you learned to **remind** yourself how you want to be treated. Then, you learned to remember how **important** customers are to your job. Finally, you learned to **visualize**, **verbalize**, and **vitalize**.

P A R T 3

The Greeting

"Only a life lived for others is a life worthwhile."

–Albert Einstein

In this part:

▶ Moment of Magic II: The Greeting

Moment of Magic II: The Greeting

Pam's excitement about improving her customer service skills led her to the Internet, where she found some interesting facts.

- ▶ Customer loyalty is worth ten times the price of a single purchase.

- ▶ A satisfied customer tells four to six other people about the experience.

- ▶ An unsatisfied customer tells eight to twelve other people.

- ▶ On average, one in four customers of a company has a complaint about it.

- ▶ The best service companies charge more, have more market share, are more profitable, and have more than double the sales growth of their competitors.

She read reports that demonstrated that the companies with the best service made more profit and were better places to work. She was amazed to see how important courteous, polite, and helpful people could be to a business.

Pam met Susan again a few days later at a local restaurant. Susan greeted Pam with a smile and shook hands firmly.

"Hi!" she said. "It's nice to see you again. Would you like a soda or coffee?"

"Water is fine," Pam said.

Then Susan began. "We've talked about Mental Psyche, so let me ask you a question. Let's say you're mentally prepared. You're ready, positive, and willing to do your job. What's the first thing you do for a customer?"

Pam thought for a couple of seconds and said, "Help the person."

"Yes," said Susan. "You want to do that. But a customer needs a proper greeting. It takes only a few moments, and it sets the tone for a customer's visit. Besides, always remember that the best moments you spend are the ones you invest in a customer. And treat every customer like she's the most important."

"Don't most people know this?" asked Pam.

"In theory they do, but they don't practice it," responded Susan. "Have you ever gone to a restaurant, clothing store, or specialty shop where the employees didn't seem to notice you, or they treated you discourteously?

"Sure," Pam answered.

Susan continued, "Let's watch the waitresses in this restaurant. What do you notice about ours and the one over there?"

"Our waitress hasn't been here yet, and she seemed fairly abrupt with the folks at the next table. The other waitress is smiling and courteous and seems to be upbeat and attentive to that couple that sat down a few minutes ago," added Pam.

"Excellent customer service people know the value of a greeting. Even if someone understands that, they still have to do it," said Susan. "Of course, a positive and proper greeting is situational. How you greet someone on the phone is a little different from what happens at an airline check-in counter. Yet, there are key ingredients."

"Such as..?"

"First, smile and make eye contact. Eye contact doesn't work on the phone, but a smile does. The smile must be genuine in either case. Next, welcome the customer. For example: 'Good morning. Welcome to ABC Company. How may I help you?' Be enthusiastic; make sure you're wearing a nametag, if appropriate, to identify yourself. Use the person's name, if you know the customer. If time permits, engage in small talk. It projects friendliness. Handle the initial inquiries politely and courteously.

"Make sure the whole greeting is appropriately prompt. Don't pounce on customers when they contact you, but don't let them become aggravated by inattention. Genuine friendliness and courtesy are very valuable.

"Not too long ago, I saw a newspaper article on the cover of the magazine section. The lead article had a picture of a herd of pigs and was titled 'The Death of Manners.' In other words, the article described how people aren't always civil today. They lack courtesy and manners. A research report on why customers leave a business said that, 68% of the time, it's because of the indifferent, rude attitude of the employees."

The best moments I spend are moments I invest in customers. Every customer is important."

"You know," Pam said, "Isn't this all learned by employees who have customer contact after a few days of being on the job?"

"It could be," agreed Susan. "The key is in the action. SuperSTAR Customer Service isn't knowledge but action. Too often, service people skip steps, because they're tired, unappreciated, stressed out, or don't know how to be courteous. SuperSTAR Customer Service people use Mental Psyche and then make the other Moments of Magic happen, like the Greeting. The result is that they engage customers positively, respectfully, and professionally and treat customers better than expected." Superstars provide uncommon kindness. There's a book by the editors of Conari Press called *Random Acts of Kindness*. The book provides ideas and examples for us to perform random acts of kindness for others without seeking a reward in return. The theory is that the recipients will pass it on, and then a trend of people helping people will gain momentum. With random acts of kindness, you quietly help others just to be friendly and nice. That's pretty cool, isn't it? Do you know what SuperSTAR Customer Service is? It's *planned* acts of kindness!

SuperSTAR Customer Service is planned acts of kindness."

"I like that. I'm beginning to understand that these Moments of Magic go together. In service, we need to take charge of our own attitude and actions. With Mental Psyche, we stay positive and focused. That translates into a friendly courteous greeting," said Pam.

"That's right," agreed Susan. "And it takes only a few moments to do. You see, all jobs require customer service. Somehow, though, people think their job is to serve food, give presentations, discuss features, fix a car, sell a product, teach a subject, or balance the books. If these things are done without a customer service focus, they're not done well. A customer service focus involves:

1. Treating any customer (internal and external) with care, courtesy, and respect.

2. Performing the task with quality.

"Too often, people just do the task. Handling a customer properly is an afterthought, and improving quality seems important only after a customer complains."

"I think I'm beginning to understand," said Pam. "There are three pharmacies in my neighborhood. I've been to each, but I use only Preston's now, because the pharmacist and staff are especially courteous. The pharmacies have the same medicines, but the pharmacist at Preston's always smiles—even as she works the register. Everything is always ready on time, and the pharmacist is also available for questions or an explanation. It's really the friendliness, promptness, and personal attention that bring me back."

Susan added, "You've described exactly what I'm talking about."

"What's next?" Pam asked. "I can't wait to review the other Moments of Magic."

"Let's slow down just a bit," said Susan. "First, you should work on Mental Psyche and the Greeting for a few days. Then, it's time you talked to Len Jones. He's the other person Joe told you about. Len will give you another perspective, and he'll fill you in on the next two Moments of Magic. So let's keep in touch. I'm confident you're on the road to becoming a SuperSTAR Customer Service person."

"Susan, thank you so much. I really appreciate your time and willingness to help. I do have a lot to work on and apply already," said Pam.

"As a thank you for your loyalty, we are offering you this hardly used pencil."

TOP TEN CUSTOMER GREETING TIPS

Put a plus sign (+) beside the things you do regularly when you greet customers. Put a circle beside any item you need to remember to do to more often to be uncommonly courteous.

____ 1. Smile. A smile needs to be genuine and natural to be effective.

____ 2. Make eye contact. Use the glance-away method. Don't lock eye balls, it's intimidating. Look at the customer a few seconds, move your eyes away, and come back.

____ 3. Acknowledge customers promptly. You can acknowledge several of them through eye contact, a wave of the hand, or a smile. Answer phone calls in three rings or less. If it takes longer add, "Thank you for waiting," to your greeting.

____ 4. Use the other person's name. If you know the customer, the first name is fine. If you don't, use Mr. or Ms.

____ 5. Give the customer your complete attention. Trying to do other things while helping a customer is a rookie mistake. Focusing on a single customer saves time and makes the customer happier.

____ 6. Make pleasant conversation: "How are you today?" "Are you having a good day?" If the customer isn't, say, "Then I will do my best to make it a bit better."

____ 7. Convey eagerness to help. Be positive and upbeat in your voice. Show enthusiasm and a sense of urgency in your efforts.

____ 8. Acknowledge people you've served before. If you make a comment about a prior contact, it makes them feel special and more loyal over time.

____ 9. Be polite and respect everyone. Use terms such as hi, good to see you, please, excuse me, thank you, sir, ma'am.

____ 10. Ask, "How may I help you today?" This begins the process of moving from the greeting to meeting needs.

Greeting Customers: Review

"Before you go, Susan," Pam said, "let me see if I can put this all together. Regardless of the work environment—positive or negative, good or bad—Mental Psyche can help you break through mediocrity and develop a positive attitude about really caring for and helping customers. Then, when you meet customers, you're prepared to serve them in the right way, a customer-focused way. The Greeting becomes an extension of Mental Psyche. Customers notice and appreciate your obvious care and concern. To the customer, there's a difference, an almost magical difference. The first two Moments of Magic set an extraordinarily positive tone with the customer. These Moments of Magic are common sense. I wonder why no one explained them to me before?"

"Maybe they're too obvious," said Susan. "People tend to look for shortcuts or an imagined secret to success." She added, "I've learned that, to be friendly, there are seven Moments of Truth you can manage in most situations:

1. Smile and make eye contact.

2. Give your name (or wear a name badge) and use the other person's name (or say sir or ma'am.)

3. Thank the customer for the opportunity to be of service by being enthusiastic, positive, and eager to help.

4. Engage in small talk, if you have time.

5. Ask a question such as, "How may I help you?"

6. Be appropriately prompt. (If you can't greet someone immediately, make eye contact and smile or thank them for waiting.)

7. Remember, courtesy is the gold standard!

"If you apply these consistently, you'll begin to create Moments of Magic for your customers through these planned acts of kindness," Susan noted. "Well, take care of yourself and don't forget – SuperSTAR Customer Service isn't knowledge but action."

> **SuperSTAR Customer Service is not about knowledge but action. Take care of the customer!"**

Moment of Magic II: The Greeting

Purpose

Begin delivering SuperSTAR Customer Service to customers with uncommon friendliness and courtesy. It takes only a few moments to get off to the right start with your customers.

Action Steps

1. Smile and make eye contact.

2. Give your name, or wear a name tag, and use the customer's name or say sir/ma'am.

3. Thank the customer for the opportunity to be of service by being enthusiastic, positive, and eager to help.

4. Engage in small talk, if you have time.

5. Ask a question like, "How may I help you?" Or, "How may I be of service to you?" Or, "Where may I direct your call?"

6. Be appropriately prompt. (If you can't greet someone immediately, make eye contact and smile, or thank them for waiting.)

7. Remember, courtesy is the gold standard!

SUPERSTAR APPLICATION 4: THE GREETING

Think of the last place of business where you spent money. How did the customer service people greet you? Use the list below to rate the people who served you. Did they follow the action steps as they waited on you?

Yes	No	
❑	❑	1. Smiled and made eye contact.
❑	❑	2. Gave their names.
❑	❑	3. Welcomed enthusiastically.
❑	❑	4. Made small talk.
❑	❑	5. Asked, "How may I help you?"
❑	❑	6. Helped you promptly.
❑	❑	7. Acted courteously.

Summary

In this part, you learned that **The Greeting** is **Moment of Magic II**. You learned that Moments of Truth in The Greeting are to **smile**, give your **name**, **thank** the customer, engage in **small talk**, ask **questions**, be **prompt**, and be **courteous**.

Meeting the Need

> **"** *Service is what life is all about."*
>
> **–Marian Wright Edelman**

In this part:

▶ Moment of Magic III: Meeting the Need

Moment of Magic III: Meeting the Need

During the next week, Pam began to apply the Moments of Magic she'd learned. She noticed that customers were more pleasant to her and that she had fewer problems. By applying Mental Psyche, she had a more enthusiastic attitude about her job. Some of her co-workers commented on how positive and upbeat she was. Pam found that the Moments of Magic worked with fellow employees, too. Energized by such positive results, she eagerly anticipated her meeting with Len, which was coming up in a few days.

Pam met Len later that week in his office. He was the manager of technical applications for a computer software company.

"Welcome," said Len warmly, as he extended his hand. "Susan and Joe have told me all about you. They like your willingness to learn, and they say you're serious about SuperSTAR Customer Service."

"I sure am," said Pam. "I'm already experiencing success on my job as a result of what I've learned. It does work, and it's fun, too. But I do have some questions."

Len sat back in his chair and smiled. "Let's get started then," he said. "I have about an hour and a half, so we'll cover one area today and another next week."

"What is the next Moment of Truth? I know it involves delivering the product or service. And I know I'm doing some of it at work, but I don't know if it's excellent or not."

Len explained that Moment of Magic III is "Meeting the Need." "It's where you explain the product, review the brief, check in the car, or do the computer repair. Remember, this is the third Moment of Magic, not the first. Without doing the other two, the best you can deliver here is mediocrity. However, this is where many customer service people start. And Meeting the Need is the area that most of us do partially well."

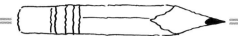

TOP TEN CUSTOMER WANTS AND NEEDS

Circle the numbers of those items that you think customers want or need. Add any others from your experience.

1. Positive, courteous, and enthusiastic employees

2. Employees who are willing to help

3. Responsive employees who serve you promptly

4. Employees who are good listeners, understand, and care

5. Employees who are neat and properly dressed for the job

6. Employees who are empowered to resolve issues or problems

7. Reliable employees who do what they say they'll do and do the job right the first time

8. Employees who are proactive and offer other help

9. Employees who follow up and go the extra mile

10. Quality products and services that perform as advertised

11. Other:_____

_____

12. Other:_____

_____

"Why do so many customer service people start with Meeting the Need?" Pam asked.

"The best way I can explain it," said Len, "is that organizations also tend to focus on Meeting the Need. Employees are taught the technical part of their jobs. Educational institutions do the same thing. For example, doctors and lawyers absorb volumes of information about their fields, but they receive minimal training in interpersonal communications or customer service strategies. The patients and clients are taken for granted. Some lack bedside manners or empathy.

"Today, marketplace changes and greater customer scrutiny are rocking these professions. For many, customer service means the difference between success and failure. Even so, employees in all types of jobs get most of their training on tasks, not on people skills. It's the people skill area where service people need to improve the most in Meeting the Need. When it comes time to type, fill orders, write reports, recite the product benefits and features, or follow company procedures, they're better prepared, but they do their jobs routinely. SuperSTAR customer service people, however, find a way to meet the need and tend to do it with some pizzazz or style. It's all about what customers want and need from us."

"Now that's what I want to learn," said Pam. "I've been served by hundreds of people who seem like zombies, just going through the motions. They seem to know what to do, but they don't do it very well."

"Remember," said Len, "You start with an exceptional attitude and a willingness to help. You greet the customer with a smile and uncommon courtesy. This is the foundation to helping."

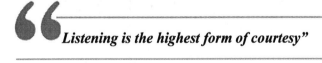

Listening is the highest form of courtesy"

Then, Len carefully led Pam through the key parts of Meeting the Need. "First, listening is critical. How can you really help a customer without it? Without it, you can only go through the motions. Remember all of what I say depends on the job and the circumstance."

"While there are many listening skills, two are crucial. First, you must want to listen. If you don't care, then it's difficult to do the job. The customer can tell by your lack of zest and attentiveness. Then, you need to clarify and demonstrate understanding by paraphrasing the customer's needs. You may have to ask a few well-placed 'what' questions to help a customer along. Some examples are: What will you do with this? What have you already tried? What do you want to accomplish? Too many service or sales people make simple errors by making assumptions."

LISTENING CHECKLIST

Rate yourself on how well you listen to customers by entering a score for each listed behavior. Use a scale of 1 to 5 where 1 is very rarely and 5 is very frequently. When finished, put a plus sign beside four of your highest rated areas. Circle the numbers of two or three areas in which you need to improve.

_____ 1. Do you want to listen?

_____ 2. Do you put other tasks out of sight and out of mind?

_____ 3. Do you make eye contact?

_____ 4. Do you minimize distractions?

_____ 5. Do you smile, nod, and otherwise encourage the speaker?

_____ 6. Do you think about what you'll say?

_____ 7. Do you ask questions to clarify what's being said?

_____ 8. Do you try to figure out why the customer is saying it?

_____ 9. Do you let the other person finish what he or she is trying to say?

_____ 10. If the person hesitates, do you encourage him or her to go on?

_____ 11. Do you paraphrase what the person says and ask if that's correct?

_____ 12. Do you withhold judgment about the issue until the customer is finished?

_____ 13. Do you listen, regardless of the customer's manner of speaking?

_____ 14. Do you listen, even when you anticipate what they'll say?

_____ 15. Do you ask questions to encourage further explanation?

_____ 16. Do you ask what's meant by some words, for clarification?

"I know what you mean by assumptions," Pam said. "Once, when I ordered concert tickets over the phone, the operator forgot to double-check my address and sent my tickets elsewhere. I was really disappointed. It was quite a mess to straighten out."

Len added, "Your comments relate to a concept that SuperSTARs embrace: Small things done consistently in strategic places create major impact."

"When I needed an oil change, I went to one of those quick change places. I wanted transmission service too, but the attendant said his location didn't do that. He said the volume of oil changes was too high to take the time, so he referred me to another store 10 miles away. I tried Cartown instead, and Joe took care of me. I've been going to him ever since. If the quick change person had taken the time to give me other options or called the other store, he might have kept my business. But he was too busy, and he rushed through everything. He created Moments of Mediocrity, not Magic, for me. More importantly, he drove a customer to a competitor—for good."

Small things done consistently in strategic places create major impact."

Len went on to say that the next Moments of Truth are critical, but so many people in customer service roles either lack the training or the willingness to do them.

"Customers like explanations, so we need to be sure they understand services they receive. For example, I took my son to the bank recently to open his first account. You can imagine what a big deal that was to him. I was very impressed with the new account representative who worked with us. She talked directly to my son, not to me, even though he had just a small amount of money. She was pleasant, knowledgeable, and thoughtful as she described his options. She made him feel important, and it made his day. Mine, too."

Pam added, "I know from personal experience how important that extra care can be. I switched my checking account because the bank was charging me for each check and didn't describe other account options. Would you believe that I learned about it from a friend? The bank employees had numerous opportunities to explain it to me."

"Once customers understand the services and their options," said Len, "they can make an informed decision. Even so, they want reassurance or support." He told Pam that SuperSTARs reassure their customers with comments such as…

▶ "I'm sure this will help you."

▶ "I think you'll really be glad you did this."

▶ "I feel sure you've made the right choice."

▶ "This should work well for you."

"It takes only a few moments, doesn't it? Then, great service people act! Knowledge isn't power; action is. They get on with it and do something to help. All talk and no walk creates Moments of Misery."

SuperSTAR Customer Service is Action

By now you should begin to see a positive difference in your customer service results. You may not have reached SuperSTAR status yet, but things should be getting better if you've taken action.

Rate yourself on your efforts to improve your level of customer service. Use a scale of 1 to 10 where 1 is little change or action and 10 is tremendous change or action. Where are you in your efforts to improve?

_____

What positive change have you made?

_____

_____

_____

What further positive changes are you willing to make?

_____

_____

_____

Pam explained that, in her quest for customer satisfaction, she's heard many promises, but many service people don't deliver. She told Len, "Some missed deadlines, forgot to return phone calls, or didn't do what they said they would do. Why, just last week I called my doctor's office to double-check a bill. The claims person couldn't answer my questions but promised to call back. I haven't heard from her, but I did get another bill! May I ask another question?"

"Sure," replied Len.

"All the things we're discussing sound great, but they seem so obvious. Aren't most people doing these things?"

"There are a couple of ways to answer your question," replied Len. "First, the Moments of Truth I've mentioned are always present in most customer service situations, even though they may be defined a little differently from one job to the next. You make misery, mediocrity, or magic by what you do. In our business, we meet customers to sell custom software. When we do so, listening, questioning, restating needs, offering options, explaining details, reassuring, and taking action are as important to the process as our technical expertise. The same is true when we have to troubleshoot problems or deal with complaints. The key is how well we do them and whether we cover all the bases. It takes customer service skills and a willingness to keep learning."

Moments of truth are always present with customers. You make these moments of misery, mediocrity, or magic by what you do and by your attitude while you do it."

"Most customer service people stop learning after the first year on the job. So, in response to your question, no. Not all people deliver Moments of Magic. They make their jobs routine and boring and settle into comfortable mediocrity.'"

Given her experiences as a customer, Pam said she'd have to agree, adding, "I think your second answer relates to attitude. Joe described the Customer Service Matrix to me when we first met."

"You're right," Len agreed. "If you don't really care or want to help, your skill becomes less useful. You go through the motions, but you don't go out of your way. Customers can sense the difference. A year ago, a new technician was assigned to my department. While he had technical ability, he upset customers with his abrasive demeanor. It took a lot of coaching on my part to get him to change. Yet on the other hand, you can have a great attitude and not be properly prepared for the task and you'll fail as well. Lack of product knowledge is a common problem."

"But that can be handled with excellence," she said. "You can tell a customer that you don't know the answer, but you can talk to someone who does or that you'll find the answer."

"That's a great point," Len conceded. "SuperSTARs are honest and willing to find a way to help the customer. I call it getting into action."

Pam said, "I have one other question. Do Moments of Magic – Mental Psyche, The Greeting, and Meeting the Need – apply to our co-workers and internal customers?"

"Pam, I see why Susan and Joe like you. We all have two types of customers—internal and external. Moments of Magic can be applied to both groups. Why would we treat fellow employees with any less CARE than external customers? It wouldn't make sense. Besides, employee satisfaction does create greater customer satisfaction. The best organizations understand this. They recognize and support their employees. Employee satisfaction does lead to better customer satisfaction."

"Can you provide good service if your company doesn't support employees?"

"Absolutely, "said Len, "remember you reviewed this with Mental Psyche. The customer doesn't or shouldn't know whether or not the company is the best place to work. An employee has the responsibility to serve a customer well, because it's the right thing to do, regardless of the work circumstances."

TOP TEN QUALITIES OF A SUPERSTAR

Circle the qualities you have. These are your strengths in providing service. Feel good about them and work on the others. Add two to three other qualities to the bottom of the list that will also help you to deliver SuperSTAR Customer Service.

1. Honest
2. Good listener
3. Courteous and polite
4. Friendly
5. Helpful
6. Team player
7. Positive and Enthusiastic
8. Knowledgeable
9. A caring person
10. Determined and persistent

_____

_____

_____

"How can employees recognize or support other employees?" asked Pam.

"There's a variety of informal ways," said Len. "Start by doing a quality job and following through. Communicate fully about what you do for them and keep them updated on your progress. Then, of course, be courteous and respectful. From time to time, write thank you notes or buy someone coffee or a soda. Also, tell others how they helped you out or just offer your help without being asked. Finally, submit their names for any company recognition programs or awards."

"Those are great ideas," she said "Thanks! I do a few of those things, but sometimes I forget to take the time."

"It takes only a few moments to satisfy an internal customer," added Len, "but we often take them for granted."

"That's true for the external customer as well," said Pam. "I've already seen how Moments of Magic take just a little more time but make a big difference."

"Well, the next Moment of Magic is Follow-through," said Len. "Let's set an appointment next week to discuss it. Then Joe asked to see you about the last one."

"That's fine, Len. I need some time to think about what we've discussed today. Thanks for all of your help. Take care."

"Now that's service! Out insurance agent is on the way!"

Meeting the Need: Review

On her drive home, Pam reviewed what she'd learned so far. The first three Moments of Magic – Mental Psyche, The Greeting, and Meeting the Need – made perfect sense. That's probably why they weren't practiced more often. The difference between winning and losing customers often comes down to little things, not grand marketing schemes. Questions like the following are very important:

▶ Do you have a positive mental attitude?

▶ Are you friendly, upbeat, and courteous?

▶ Are you skilled enough to do your job well?

While technical skills vary from job to job, communication skills for customer satisfaction are the same on any job. Moments of Magic III: Meeting the Need involves:

▶ Listening   ▶ Explaining things

▶ Asking questions   ▶ Reassuring

▶ Restating the need   ▶ Taking action

▶ Offering options

Management's role is to provide appropriate training and support for employees to be their best. Excellent organizations do this well.

However, people who provide customer service must not use poor management as an excuse for poor service, because the customers suffer. Delivering SuperSTAR Customer Service requires a CARE attitude that can overcome almost any obstacle. Mental Psyche reminds service people to CARE for customers by using a quick process to help them stay mentally prepared. The Greeting shows your caring attitude and concern by demonstrating courtesy and friendliness. Meeting the Need is the way to exhibit competence and a bias for action to really help the customer.

"I wonder ..." thought Pam out loud. "Is Joe really that good? Are Susan and Len that good, too? They seem so knowledgeable and nice."

The next morning, she called Joe's supervisor. She found out the dealership receives many calls and letters from customers who compliment Joe. What they seem to like most is that he's friendly, thorough, honest, and he really cares.

The manager commented, "Joe's the best. While he doesn't have the most technical knowledge about cars or trucks, he does know people. He always talks about "customer time" – that's his priority. The customers trust that he'll help them out in any way he can. He's always promoting customer rights with me. Yet, Joe's effectiveness goes beyond that. He also works well with other employees and makes a special effort to help them. Because of his teamwork attitude, he receives lots of support internally from the office, sales people, and technicians.

"I could go on and on, but Joe's results speak for themselves. Nearly all of his customers are repeats or referrals, and his schedule is usually full. His customer satisfaction rating is among the best, and he's won numerous awards from our automobile manufacturers. Joe's a CARE customer service person, and we're really glad to have him."

Pam thanked the manager for his comments. She hung up the phone, sat back in her chair, and smiled. While she expected some positive comments, she was impressed by the praise and recognition Joe's supervisor gave him. Joe was making a difference. Moments of Magic work! He was a SuperSTAR!

Pam thought back to her oil change experience with Joe. While it was only one encounter, Joe excelled. He was effective, friendly, courteous, prompt, and he followed through. She recalled the service person at the last dealership she tried. He was nothing like Joe.

Later that day, Pam made calls to learn more about Susan and Len. Both their supervisors gave them outstanding references and accolades, too. She was impressed. She wanted to be thought of in that way and became determined to make it happen.

Moment of Magic III: Meeting the Need

Purpose

Deliver SuperSTAR Customer Service to help customers solve problems or to meet or exceed their needs or wants.

Action Steps

1. Listen to the customer.

2. Ask questions to clarify needs.

3. Restate the needs to demonstrate understanding.

4. Offer options when identifying solutions. (Choices empower customers.)

5. Explain all necessary information.

6. Reassure the customers about their choices or decisions.

7. Take action on the customer's need or decision: Do something positive to help.

SuperSTAR Application 5: Meeting the Need

Identify three internal and three external customers and what they need from you. Answer the question below to help you help them.

Internal Customers

1. _____
2. _____
3. _____

How can you use Moments of Magic I, II, and III to provide better service?

_____

_____

_____

_____

External Customers

1. _____
2. _____
3. _____

How can you use Moments of Magic I, II, and III to provide better service?

_____

_____

_____

_____

Summary

In this part, you learned that **Meeting the Need** is **Moment of Magic III**. You learned that the Moments of Truth in Meeting the Need include **listening**, asking **questions**, **restating** the need, offering **options**, **explaining** things, **reassuring** the customer, and taking **action**.

Follow-Through

It's one of the most beautiful compensations in life, that no man can sincerely help another without helping himself."

– Ralph Waldo Emerson

In this part:

▶ Moment of Magic IV: Follow-through

Moment of Magic IV: Follow-through

It was time to meet with Len again to discuss the next Moment of Magic. Pam had received a thank you note and email from Len since their last meeting and a voicemail message confirming their upcoming appointment.

She smiled as she greeted him in his office. "It's good to see you again. Thanks for your time. I really appreciate it. How are you doing?"

"I'm glad to invest the time, especially with people who are eager to learn. I'm doing fine."

"Well, to begin…" started Pam, "I have a confession to make. I called and talked to your supervisor, as well as Joe's and Susan's. I just had to find out…"

"That's fine," Len said. "I hope you found what you were looking for."

"I just wanted to hear what others had to say about whether or not you guys were really that good." She added, "To tell you the truth, I expected them to say you were good, but their compliments went way beyond that. Not only did they praise you, they said your customers routinely do the same."

"It's nice to get the recognition. Thank you!" said Len. "However, creating customer loyalty matters more. Customers are the reason for our jobs. Make them happy and the business is successful, and so are the employees. I was told long ago that, if you want to be successful, look at how people do their jobs, and then do it better, faster, or different. SuperSTAR Customer Service works because it's a common-sense game plan that helps in any situation."

SuperSTAR Customer Service works because it's a common-sense game plan of five Moments of Magic that help in any situation."

"How did you learn Moments of Magic?" asked Pam.

"In a variety of ways," he responded. "Classes on customer service and communication helped, as well as plain old experience. But Joe really taught me the five Moments of Magic and how to use them. As his customer, I was so impressed with his service that I asked him to share his secret—which he did, over time. Are you ready to discuss Moment of Magic IV: Follow-through?"

"I sure am," she said, with the interest of a student who'd really begun to understand her homework. "In fact, I remember when I made an appointment with Joe. He called later to confirm, sent me a thank you note after the service was completed, and just the other day, I received a survey card in the mail. I also received information about special services from him in my email. And then, you and Susan contacted me after our meetings, too. Is follow-up important with the internal customer, too?"

"We'll not only get your luggage back, we'll fill it full of goodies."

"Follow-through is an area where many service people fail with external or internal customers," Len explained. "The result is many unnecessary Moments of Misery. Let me give you an example. I once received a call from a salesman selling tickets to a seminar with a nationally known speaker. He sounded energetic, so I made an appointment with the salesman. Two days later, I received this beautiful card."

Len showed Pam a 3- by 5-inch card with a sunset background across a still lake. He flipped the card over. There was a note on the back that read:

> Len,
>
> I look forward to meeting you soon!
>
> Sincerely,
> Bob

Len continued, "I really like this card. Here, let me read the quote on the front by Anatole France. 'To accomplish great things, we must not only act but also dream, not only plan but also believe.' Isn't that inspiring? I got this card and thought, 'I can't wait to meet this guy and then hear the speaker.' However, I'm still waiting. He never showed up or called again. It's been over two years. I keep the card because I like it, but it's also a reminder of the importance of Follow-through."

"So the guy started out right, but didn't finish. He obviously didn't deliver SuperSTAR Customer Service," Pam said. "Tell me, what's involved?"

"Follow-through often requires a little extra effort. It's a way of giving added value. It builds long-lasting customer satisfaction and repeat business. It starts with a sincere 'thank you' to a customer. Have you ever not received a 'thank you' from a person providing service to you?"

"Nearly every time I went to Bear Grocery Store," Pam chimed in. "They don't seem to know the words. Lately, I've been going across the street to Bear's competitor, Apple Foods. They're always friendly and find ways to go out of their way to show that they appreciate my business."

Len said, "You're right when you describe friendly behavior as going above and beyond to show appreciation. Friendly is different from nice. Nice is passive or reactive, and you tend to wait for the customer to seek or ask for help. SuperSTARs are friendly. Friendly means you're proactive. You look for customers and make an effort to help them before they ask."

"Wow! I like that," Said Susan.

'Nice' is passive or reactive, and you tend to wait for customers to seek or ask for help. SuperSTARs are friendly. Friendly means you're proactive. You look for customers and make an effort to help them before they ask."

–Rick Conlow

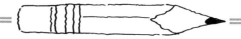

TOP TEN WAYS TO HELP INTERNAL CUSTOMERS

Circle the number of any actions you take now. Put a plus sign beside any you want to do. Add one other action you've done that isn't on the list. Bring moments of magic to internal customers too.

1. Ask how you can serve them more effectively.

2. Keep your promises or commitments.

3. Send a thank you email, text message, or note to those who help you.

4. Check back to make sure everything is okay.

5. Ask if you can help before you're asked for help.

6. Bring them information that would be helpful.

7. Treat them with the utmost respect and courtesy.

8. Offer them a soda, coffee, or water.

9. Respond to any requests for help promptly.

10. Communicate regularly to keep updated on their needs.

11. Other: _____

Len added, "It takes just a moment to show extra appreciation to customers by using comments like:

▶ 'Have a nice day.'

▶ 'Take care of yourself.'

▶ 'Please come again.'

▶ 'We appreciate your business.'

▶ 'Thanks so much for coming.'

▶ 'I look for toward to seeing you again.'

▶ 'Thanks again for your business.'"

"Next, all phone calls or emails must be returned promptly. Too many people don't return phone calls or emails and have out-of-date outgoing messages. Nearly 70% of business calls don't reach the intended person. Failing to return a call or email is rude and unprofessional. Get back to customers the same day, if possible. If you have voicemail, it's crucial to check it often. Too often, people don't check for messages, use voicemail as a screening device, or leave the wrong outgoing message. These are all Moments of Misery for customers.

"A computer sales person I know has a phenomenal addition to her voice messages. At the end of her greeting, she says, 'I promise that I'll get back to you within four hours,' and she does! Her customers appreciate her sense of urgency."

When you send email messages, always have a topic. Write it as a letter, include bullet points, stick to the point, sign off with a sincerely yours type statement, and include all of your contact information. Too many emails contain poor grammar, no topic, and rambling bits of information.

"Wow! Even emails can deliver SuperSTAR Customer Service!" Pam exclaimed.

"Absolutely," said Len. "Follow-through is an area that can clearly distinguish your efforts. But there's an additional principle that creates Moments of Magic: Under-promise and over-deliver. Take Joe at the dealership. He has his customers' cars washed and vacuumed after each visit. He doesn't mention it. He just has it done. It's always a pleasant surprise. A hotel I stayed at last week turned the covers down on the bed in the evening and left a nice note with a mint on the table by the bedside. Later, the manager called to make sure everything was okay."

Len told Pam there are a number of ways service people can demonstrate their desire to go the extra mile. "Send information articles to the customer. Refer them to someone who can help them, if you can't. Share other ideas that might help them. Hold seminars to educate them.

"Obviously, what you do depends on the situation and the job. Most people who serve customers can put the final touch on a customer's experience by sending a thank you note or by expressing appreciation in a genuine manner or checking back to make sure everything is okay. They can also ask for feedback to be of further service with statements like:

▶ 'Is everything okay?'

▶ 'How are we doing?'

▶ 'Is there anything else I can do for you?'

▶ 'How else can I help you today?'"

"Questions like these express CARE and concern."

Pam considered that and then said, "Len, these aren't new things. They've been said before. The problem is that too few people really do them. People lack either the skill or the will. In my search for customer service, I've seen service people consistently handle Moments of Truth with mediocrity or misery. Few perform magically, although I'm learning from you, Joe, and Susan that they can."

"Anybody can become a service SuperSTAR, if they CARE about others and are willing to learn about Moments of Magic," said Len.

"I really appreciate the time you're taking to help me," Pam said. "It's been a real education. I do have a question I need help with, though."

"What is it?" asked Len.

"How do you know when you're delivering SuperSTAR Customer Service?"

"You know. You'll become proactive and passionate about really helping people. Your customers will start treating you differently. I'll tell you what. Call Joe again. There's one more Moment of Magic for you to learn. Joe's a master at it. Before you meet him again, arrive at the dealership a little early. Walk around and watch Joe and the others work with customers. You'll see how everything fits together. You'll begin to discover the depth involved in SuperSTAR Customer Service."

Wow! I like that," Said Susan.

Anyone who's willing to learn and implement Moments of Magic can deliver SuperSTAR Customer Service."

Follow-through: Review

That evening Pam began to review what she'd learned. The objective of Moment of Magic I: Mental Psyche is to help service people feel positive and enthusiastic about helping customers. Moment of Magic II: The Greeting focuses on meeting customers with the utmost friendliness and professionalism. Moment of Magic III: Meeting the Need involves listening and helping customers with a need or a problem. Moment of Magic IV: Follow-through simply requires finishing strong, ensuring that customers are happy. Follow-through involves:

- ▶ Saying "thank you."

- ▶ Doing what you said you would.

- ▶ Sending thank you notes or letters or emails.

- ▶ Showing appreciation with a positive comment.

- ▶ Returning calls or emails promptly.

- ▶ Making sure to under-promise and over-deliver.

- ▶ Asking to be of further assistance.

Pam wondered what the details of the last Moment of Magic would be, but her stomach interrupted her thoughts. It was dinner time. She sailed in to a local fast food restaurant for a bite to eat. The place was packed with noisy, restless commuters. As she waited in line to give her order, her thoughts turned to her meetings with Susan and Len. At first, she didn't notice the other people around her. But she couldn't help but overhear the comments people were making about the counter person one line over.

Pam turned to look. After observing her for a few moments, her eyes lit up. The young woman was a true delight. She smiled and greeted her customer with, "How are you doing? What will it be tonight?" Once she received the order, she summarized it, asked if he wanted dessert, and said, "It will be right up." She then dashed over to the fries, encouraging fellow workers along the way and got two sodas started (one for the next counter person). When she returned, she bagged the order, took the money and made change. As she did so, she added, "Hope you enjoy it. Have a great night and come back real soon. Thank you."

Pam thought to herself that, in a few short moments, this person had completed each SuperSTAR Moment of Magic, including Follow-through. She approached the next customer with the same enthusiasm – a wonderful demonstration of Mental Psyche. Her line moved quickly and the customers walked away smiling. She was a SuperSTAR, indeed.

Pam took note of the other counter personnel. They did the same job, but it looked different. Low-key and robotic, they weren't necessarily bad, just mediocre. Their customers walked away with little expression on their faces.

"Awesome," Pam thought. "What a contrast! The counter person making such a favorable impression on her customers really cares and is delivering Moments of Magic. She probably doesn't even know it. She seems to enjoy her job and treats both internal and external customers with courtesy, respect, and care. She's a SuperSTAR!"

Pam slipped into the other line to place her order. After she was served, she told the counter person what a pleasure it was to be helped by someone who cared. "Thank you!" she said and winked at her.

As Pam left the restaurant, she saw that this SuperSTAR was still as cheerful as when she first noticed her. There was a sort of magic to it all. She couldn't wait to visit with Joe about the last Moment of Magic.

HOW DO CUSTOMERS SEE YOU?

Re-read the description of the counter help at the fast food restaurant. Then answer the questions below.

What did this customer service person do that was exceptional?

_____

_____

How do you think your customers would describe you?

_____

_____

Moment of Magic IV: Follow-through

Purpose

Go the extra mile to ensure that the customer is happy. Go above and beyond to add that extra touch that keeps the customer loyal.

Action Steps

1. Say "thank you" to the customer every time with sincerity.

2. Do what you say you'll do—and then some!

3. Send thank you notes or letters or emails of appreciation.

4. Add a personal comment that you appreciate the business.

5. Return phone calls or messages or emails promptly.

6. Under-promise, over-deliver, do a little more, and be creative.

7. Ask to be of further service.

Customers learn more from poor service than they do from products or pricing."

SuperSTAR Application 6: Follow-through

The six Moments of Magic in Follow-through are listed below. Identify two ways that you can apply each of these to your job and the customers you serve. Then add another category that applies to your job.

1. Say "thank you." For example, "Thank you for coming in, I hope to see you soon."

2. Send thank you notes or letters or emails. For example, a grocery store could put thank you notes in the bag signed by the cashier.

3. Return calls or emails promptly. Make a commitment in your voicemail message. For example, "Hi, this is Rick. Sorry I'm unable to take your call. Please leave a detailed message, and I promise to get back to you within 4 hours."

4. Add a personal comment of appreciation. For example, "It was good to see you again. Have a nice vacation and come see me when you get back."

5. Under-promise and over-deliver. For example, "I can have that to you by tomorrow noon." Then get it to them in the morning.

6. Ask to be of further service. For example, "A nice sweater would go well with these slacks." Or, "Did you know we have a sale on?"

7. Other: _____

Summary

In this part, you learned that **Follow-Through** is **Moment of Magic IV**. You learned that Moments of Truth in Meeting the Need include saying **thank you**, **doing** what you say, **sending** notes or emails, **adding** a personal comment, **returning** calls and messages, **under-promising and over-delivering**, and asking to be of **further service**.

6

Handling

Problems

> "To care for anyone else enough to make their problems one's own is ever the beginning of one's own ethical development."

–Felix Adler

In this part:

▶ Moments of Magic V: Handling Problems

Moments of Magic V: Handling Problems

Pam scheduled an appointment with Joe for additional work on her car. He sent her a reminder note, but she called to confirm and arranged to meet him after work.

On the day of the appointment, she dropped her car off at Cartown. Joe greeted her with his usual charm, even though he was extremely busy. After leaving her car, Pam began to concentrate on her own workday. On the shuttle ride to work, she made final preparations for her day. She'd already sent reminder notes to others about the training session she needed to do but needed to double-check some details. Then, she considered how she could add value to the service she would deliver to her customers that day.

Later that morning, Joe called to recommend rotating the tires and to explain what he'd done with her car. He inspired such confidence that she couldn't help but feel good. She arrived back at Cartown a few minutes before closing, as Len suggested. The place was really hopping with customers anxious to be on their way home. Employees seemed to enjoy helping them. But Pam noted many other positives:

▶ The building was immaculate—free from oil stains, trash, and cigarette butts littering the ground.

▶ Signage focused on customers or employee appreciation.

▶ The customer lounge was clean and comfortable with recent magazines, coffee and soda, snacks, and a Wi-Fi hotspot.

▶ No customers were left unattended. She was asked twice if she needed help.

Pam noticed Joe in the service aisle. He was friendly, prompt, and upbeat. He shook hands with all of his customers. They smiled and often joked with him. Nearly all said they looked forward to seeing him again. She knew Joe would send them a thank you note and a customer service survey. Joe truly was a SuperSTAR. Pam's attention was suddenly drawn to the loud and angry comments of a customer. The comments were directed at Joe! Joe listened, but also appeared to be very focused on the customer as he reviewed some paperwork with him. Within moments, the customer calmed down. A couple of minutes later, he smiled, shook hands with Joe and left. Joe moved on, flashing his usual grin as if nothing had happened.

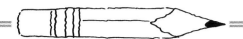

TOP TEN CUSTOMER COMPLAINTS

Complaints tend to be specific by company or industry. But those in the list below represent common categories. Check the top three that you've observed at your own workplace. Put a circle beside any that you have to make an effort to avoid in your own work.

_____ 1. Employee had a poor or negative attitude.

_____ 2. Employee exhibited lack of courtesy.

_____ 3. Employee was too aggressive and bothered the customer.

_____ 4. Employee acted as if too busy to help.

_____ 5. Customer had to wait too long—to be greeted or to be helped.

_____ 6. Employee lacked knowledge of products or services.

_____ 7. Employee was unwilling to help.

_____ 8. Employee had poor listening skills.

_____ 9. Customer couldn't find the product wanted, or it was out of stock.

_____ 10. Employee displayed lack of attentiveness to the customer.

Later that night, as Pam and Joe sat at a nearby restaurant to discuss the day's events, Pam asked about the angry customer.

"Customers who complain or get upset fall into the fifth Moment of Magic area," Joe explained. "That's the last one you need to learn."

"Yes, Len told me to ask you about it," Pam said.

"It's not always easy to handle difficult situations like the one I had today. But we must remember an underlying principle of excellent customer service: Exceed the customer's expectations. Two customers might react differently to identical situations, depending on their outlooks on life and the things that are going on for them at the moment. Our job is to help regardless of the situation. The man today was upset because we had to order a part to complete his truck repairs. I'd called a couple of times but was unable to reach him. I left a message each time, plus I left him a message on our Customer Care line, where he could call to get his status."

"Customers don't care about all that, Joe," interrupted Pam. "They just want the vehicle done right and on time."

> *Remember an underlying principle of excellent customer service: Exceed the customer's expectations.*

"You're partly right," Joe continued. "The customer got angry, because his truck wasn't finished, and it was an inconvenience for him. I responded by listening effectively, acknowledging his feelings, and then telling him he had a right to be upset and that I was sorry he was inconvenienced. When I did this, did you notice he didn't yell anymore? He wasn't completely satisfied, but he did calm down. Listening is the highest form of courtesy. I call that 'deal with the person first before you deal with the problem.' If you ignore the person and just jump right in to fix the problem, the customer might get angrier and leave with stronger negative feelings. You don't want that. An unhappy customer tells eight to ten other people. Positive word-of-mouth advertising is worth its weight in gold. Just think of new movie releases. How a movie is received by those first audiences across the country makes all the difference in the world. People talk, and news travels fast."

> *Listening is the highest form of courtesy.*

"There's a two-step process for handling complaints," said Joe. "First, deal with the person. Then—and only then—deal with the complaint."

"So what did you do next?"

"Remember, until you demonstrate that you understand and care, customers stay upset," added Joe. "Then, solve the problem. I asked him more questions about his situation and then suggested a plan to help. Plus, I gave him a few options. People like choices, so give them some. I told him we checked around town for the part, but no one had it, so I ordered it from our supplier, and we'd have it in two days. I then explained my attempts to contact him at the number he gave me plus our CCS line. He apologized for yelling at me at that point. His options were to schedule a return visit then or wait for me to call him when the part arrived. I took action by suggesting he schedule an appointment then so I could reserve a loaner car for him. And so, that's what we did. I apologized again and he left thanking me for the help."

First, deal with the person. Then, deal with the complaint"

Pam was curious. "Does this work all of the time?"

"Certainly not," said Joe. "It does work most of the time, because most customers are nice, agreeable people. However, some customers get more upset. Then, there are four other things to try."

"What do you mean?" Pam asked.

Joe explained that, if dealing with the person/dealing with the problem doesn't work, don't repeat it – try a different approach.

"But, how do you know if it isn't working?" Pam wanted to know.

"Well, first of all, the customer gets more upset—perhaps even louder. She may also begin to repeat herself and get more demanding. If you use the same approach again, you'll go in circles, which adds fuel to the fire." Joe defined.

"That would be frustrating to both the employee and the customer," Pam interjected.

Joe nodded. "You're exactly right. That's where these four methods come in. However, use only two of the four and pick the method that best meets your customer's need. For customers who are extremely demanding or overbearing, be assertive, direct, and get to the point with them. I call it the Lion Method. Stay courteous and respectful, but act quickly and decisively."

"Wouldn't that cause a confrontation?" asked Pam in surprise.

"Not if you're respectful and courteous as you get to the point and do something. Remember, give other people what they want, and you'll get what you want. Use the Lion Method only with dominant, confrontational individuals. Use the St. Bernard Method with amiable customers. They need a service representative who'll come to their rescue. They aren't as direct as customers who require the Lion Method. Instead, they worry about problems  and get emotional. When they get angry, they need a friend who'll listen and empathize. So, take the time to do that. Tell them you're on their side. Express your concern and desire to help. Apologize again and tell them you have some ideas that may help. Do you see the difference between the two customers I've discussed?"

"Yes. The first is more results-oriented, while the second is more social- or feelings-oriented," Pam replied.

"Now, there's a third type," added Joe. "I use the Fox method for customers who are analytical, like my customer today. If you remember, I had to show him the paperwork and my time log for phone contacts and follow-up. Fox customers aren't as expressive as Lions or St. Bernards. But they want a plan and a step-by-step process to solve their problem. So, give it to them. Tell them you'll review their situation thoroughly, point by point. Go over the paperwork and give them options."

"I like the animal analogy. It's easy to remember," said Pam. "Why do you think these methods work?"

Joe paused briefly to consider her question. "They work, because you're meeting customers in their world, not yours. These approaches may vary, but they each express a caring attitude. However, if you try them on a customer and can't solve the problem, then you must get help That's the fourth method. First, try to get a manager to help out, but if none is available, try another employee. Always update the person offering to help before introducing the customer to her. This way, the helper starts out informed, and the customer doesn't have to repeat everything."

Four Additional Methods to Handle Complaints

1. The **Lion** Method—Be assertive and direct.

2. The **St. Bernard** Method—Be attentive and ultra-kind.

3. The **Fox** Method—Be analytical and thoughtful.

4. When all else fails, get **help**.

"This means you can't satisfy everyone," Pam concluded.

Joe acknowledged that this is probably true, even though the SuperSTAR Customer Service goal is 100% customer satisfaction and loyalty. "An unblemished record is possible for a given day, week, or month, but unlikely over a lifetime," he said. "Remember, customers complain for their own reasons, justified or not. Sometimes they're right, and sometimes they're wrong. I don't agree with two customer service rules that some experts promote: Rule No.1--The customer is always right; and Rule No. 2--If the customer is wrong, reread Rule No.1. These rules make it difficult for employees to do what's right."

" *Customers are always the customer, even when they're wrong."*

"Instead, I say, 'the customer is always the customer, even when they're wrong.' Sometimes, you may have to say 'no' when customers are unreasonable. Treat the customer with respect and courtesy at all times, even in difficult situations. Using these methods of handling problems gives you a fantastic opportunity to make an unhappy customer a happy one. The only exception is the rare instance when a customer gets verbally abusive or hints at physical abuse. If this happens, end the contact quickly and get help."

"I hope I never encounter anyone like that," Pam said.

"It doesn't happen often, but we must be aware," assured Joe.

"We've talked it over and we've decided that you must not really be a customer."

Joe went on, "We must concentrate on delivering SuperSTAR Customer Service by using the tools of Mental Psyche, The Greeting, Meeting the Need, Follow-through, and Handling Problems. If you do these things, you'll avoid five common Moments of Misery."

"What are those?" asked Pam.

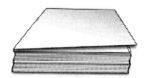

"The first is the 'Let me get the paperwork' ploy. The customer has a problem, so the service person tells him to wait or to hold the phone while she checks the records. So, she keeps him waiting in the customer lounge until his coffee's cold or on the phone until he's started to doze off. Sometimes, she never gets back to him as promised.

"I call the second Moment of Misery the 'Village Idiot' method. The customer service person acts completely brain-dead. He lacks initiative and responsibility and plays dumb, passes the buck, or criticizes others for the problem. They say it's not their job. Customers hate this trick. Service people must help customers, even if the problem doesn't fit into their area of expertise or responsibility. At the least, they can find someone else to help or make a referral. It's everyone's job to satisfy a customer, from the CEO to the mailperson."

"The third Moment of Misery is the 'Promises, Promises' approach. In this case, when the customer has a problem, the service person smiles, shakes hands, promises the moon and, with gusto, says, 'Trust me.' The customer leaves believing the problem is resolved, but nothing happens."

"What are the next two Moments of Misery?"

"The fourth is the 'Insult Comic Approach.' These service people are rude, sarcastic, and discourteous. Some research claims that the main reason customers flee a business for the competition is due to the indifferent, poor attitude of its employees!

"And the last Moment of Misery is the Kamikaze Tactic to customer service. These service people are ruthless in driving customers away. For example, they:

▶ Ignore the customer.

▶ Tell the customer they don't need customers like them.

▶ Use off-color language or humor.

▶ Threaten the customer.

Moments of Misery: Avoid these at all costs!

- ▶ The "Let Me Get the Paperwork" Ploy
- ▶ The Village Idiot Method
- ▶ The "Promises, Promises" Approach
- ▶ The Insult Comic Attitude
- ▶ The Kamikaze Tactic

Pam chimed in, "You know, Joe, as you described these Moments of Misery, I remembered incidents just like them. In my travels, I've had sales people, clerks, managers, and technicians create misery for me and for others. None of it had to happen. Things like poor language, lying, rudeness, lack of follow-through, lack of product knowledge, not paying attention, and slow service can all be avoided."

"SuperSTAR Customer Service people understand that their approach affects their success," Joe pointed out. "My industry is extremely competitive, but what industry isn't? If I can demonstrate competence, skill, and a caring attitude, customers come back. Besides, it's the right thing to do, isn't it? Treat people better than they expect to be treated. Give them what they want or a little more."

"And they give you what you want," added Pam. "Joe, I want to thank you for all your help. As I've watched you work with customers, I've learned a lot. Our conversations have helped tremendously, too. My meetings with Susan and Len were also valuable. I appreciate the time."

"No problem," he said. "Let's keep in touch. Let me add one other thing. True SuperSTAR Customer Service isn't the knowledge but the action. The real test of understanding is in sharing and teaching others, so spread the word."

Handling Problems: Review

That night, Pam wrote thank you letters to Joe, Susan, and Len. She smiled as she thought about the five approaches she would use to create SuperSTAR Customer Service for her customers. She knew that problems were inevitable when dealing with people. But she felt more confident that she could handle them.

Pam took a sheet of paper and wrote out the common complaints her department received. She also detailed how she would handle them, beginning with:

Deal with the person

▶ Listen

▶ Make a feeling statement

▶ Apologize

Deal with the problem

▶ Fact find

▶ Offer options to the customer

▶ Take action

She considered past customers and thought about which ones fit the Lion, St. Bernard, and Fox methods. If only she'd known these approaches before, she thought. But now she has a game plan that really works. She knows how to create satisfied customers and that it's her choice. While her search for excellent customer service seems to have ended, she knows that it's really just beginning.

Moments of Magic V: Handling Problems

Purpose

Satisfy customers who have problems and keep them coming back.

Action Steps

1. Deal with the person.

   ▷ Listen to the concern. After listening, say, "What I hear you saying is…"

   ▷ Make a feeling statement about the concern. "I can see this is an inconvenience for you."

   ▷ Apologize. "I'm sorry this happened."

2. Deal with the problem.

   ▷ Fact find and get additional information, if needed. "May I ask a few questions?"

   ▷ Offer options. "What we can do is A or B. Which would you prefer?"

   ▷ Take action. "Excellent choice. I think this will take care of things. Let's set it in motion now."

3. Try one of these approaches, if the first two steps don't work

   ▷ Lion Method -- with domineering people

   ▷ St. Bernard Method -- with amiable people

   ▷ Fox Method -- with analytical people

4. Listen to the customer. If none of the above works, get help!

5. Always remember: The customer is always the customer, even if he's wrong.

6. Go the extra mile with Moment of Magic IV: Follow-through.

 Help other people get what they want, and you'll get what you want."

–Bob Conklin

SuperSTAR Application 7:
Handling Problems

Identify four customer problems or concerns that you have to address. Then write out how you can help. Remember to deal with the person first.

1. _____
   _____
   _____
   _____

2. _____
   _____
   _____
   _____

3. _____
   _____
   _____
   _____

4. _____
   _____
   _____
   _____

Summary

In this part, you learned that **Handling Problems** is **Moment of Magic V**. You learned to **deal with the person** first, and then to **deal with the complaint**. Next, you learned the **Lion**, **St. Bernard**, and **Fox** methods and to **get help** when needed. Finally, you learned to avoid common **Moments of Misery**.

APPENDIX

SuperSTAR Customer Service

Pam was committed to what she'd learned and began to apply SuperSTAR Customer Service to her job. She began to benefit from significant changes in her outlook and performance. First, she now has less stress. Her job seems easier. She knows how to keep herself positive, customers seem more cooperative, and she has fewer problems.

Second, her co-workers help her out more. She treated them with respect and courtesy before, but now they work together better as a team. Third, her customers are happier, and they show it through their personal comments and letters. Even without this evidence, they seem friendlier and more eager to see her.

Finally, but certainly not least important, she feels better about herself. While she didn't lack self-esteem or self-confidence before, she now has the assurance that she is doing the right things. She has become a SuperSTAR Customer Service person. She concluded that the changes she made in five areas resulted in favorable customer response.

At a meeting at her job, Pam shared her observations and learning with co-workers and handed out a SuperSTAR Customer Service Model that Joe had given her. Then she reviewed the model with them using the following notes as guidelines.

Mental Psyche

Make a commitment to be positive and customer-focused, regardless of how others feel. Self-manage your own attitude by visualizing, verbalizing, and vitalizing your efforts every day. See it, say it, and do it!

The Greeting

Provide courteous, friendly, and respectful service. Doing so creates more courteous, friendly, and respectful customers. Smile; greet customers promptly with sincere enthusiasm.

Meeting the Need

Paying attention, asking good questions, listening effectively, and being other-centered (not self-centered) build lasting customer relationships and put you in a position to help customers the way they want to be helped

Follow-through

Go the extra mile to be a little better than, faster than, and different from others mean higher customer retention. Say thanks with care, send follow-up notes, if appropriate, ask to be of further service, and put an exclamation point on your service. It's about pride, isn't it?

Handling Problems

Maintain a professional and caring demeanor when handling complaints or difficult customers. Deal with the person first, and then deal with the problems. You can use other tools like the Lion, Fox, and St Bernard methods, or you can get help, if needed. Remember that the customer is always the customer. Then follow up brilliantly.

The next day, Pam's boss called her in for a meeting.

"You know, Pam," she said, "I'm impressed with your efforts this year. Our customer loyalty survey results are up significantly over last year and many of our guests have called me to express their appreciation. You've earned a promotion to store manager, and I want to enroll you in advanced leadership training. Congratulations! We'd also like you to lead an internal effort to help everyone in our organization do what you've done to increase customer satisfaction and loyalty."

Pam was pleased and proud. She'd learned to deliver SuperSTAR Customer Service through the five Moments of Magic, and the results were… well, magical. Her efforts had been rewarded, but she understood that the real magic would come from sharing the five Moments of Magic with others. She looked forward to the journey.

> **"** *SuperSTAR Customer Service: The greatest magic is to help customers and then others to learn to do it.* **"**

SuperSTAR Application 8:
My SuperSTAR Plan

Describe the actions you'll take to apply SuperSTAR Customer Service on your job. Then, review your plan with your supervisor and a co-worker. Finally, act! Deliver Moments of Magic to your customers.

What I've learned or relearned:

_____

_____

_____

Identify how you'll implement Moments of Magic with customers (be as specific as possible):

Mental Psyche: _____

_____

The Greeting: _____

_____

Meeting the Need: _____

_____

Follow-through: _____

_____

Handling Problems: _____

_____

Name _____ Date _____

SuperSTAR Customer Service: Summary

A brief summary of SuperSTAR Customer Service: How really to care for customers by keeping a positive attitude and creating Moments of Magic that leave customers more than satisfied.

▶ Keep a positive attitude.

Use Mental Psyche to be other-centered not self-centered to focus on the customer. The first step to being a superstar has nothing to do with the customer; it has everything to do with you.

▶ Be proactive.

Greet, Meet the Need, Follow Through, and Handle Problems positively and professionally with every customer every time.

Begin with:

Moment of Magic I: **Mental Psyche**	**Moment of Magic II:** **The Greeting**
1. Acknowledge feelings.	1. Smile and make eye contact.
2. Remind yourself how you want to be treated.	2. Give your name and use the customer's name.
3. Remember the customer's importance.	3. Thank the customer by being enthusiastic.
4. Visualize—see it!	4. Engage in small talk.
5. Verbalize—say it!	5. Ask, "How may I help you?"
6. Vitalize—do it!	6. Be appropriately prompt.
7. Take action!	7. Remember, courtesy is like gold!

To be all you can be, you must dream of being more."

–Arlene Lenarz

If Things Go Well...

Moment of Magic III:
Meeting the Need

1. Listen.

2. Ask questions to clarify.

3. Restate for understanding.

4. Offer options.

5. Explain.

6. Reassure the customer.

7. Take action.

Moment of Magic IV:
Follow-Through

1. Thank the customer.

2. Do what you say you will.

3. Send notes, letters, or emails.

4. Add a personal comment.

5. Return messages and calls.

6. Under-promise, over-deliver.

7. Ask to be of further service.

If Things Go Wrong...

Moment of Magic V:
Handling Problems

1. Deal with the person.

2. Deal with the problem.

3. If necessary, try the Lion, St. Bernard, or Fox approach.

4. If none of the above work, get help.

5. The customer is always the customer—even when the customer is wrong.

6. Go the extra mile with follow-through.

SuperSTAR Customer Service Inventory

Rate how well you apply Moments of Magic. Do this periodically. Also, ask your boss, peers, and customers to rate you. Circle the number that best indicates how frequently you use each of the following customer service behaviors:

5 = Very frequently   4 = Frequently   3 = Neither frequently nor infrequently
2 = Infrequently   1 = Very infrequently

Mental (Psyche)

1. Acknowledge your feelings.   1 2 3 4 5

2. Remind yourself how you want to be treated.   1 2 3 4 5

3. Remember the importance of the customer.   1 2 3 4 5

4. Visualize excellent service—see it!   1 2 3 4 5

5. Verbalize it's the right thing to do—say it!   1 2 3 4 5

6. Vitalize it with a smile for the next customer—do it!   1 2 3 4 5

The Greeting

1. Smile and make eye contact.   1 2 3 4 5

2. Give your name and use the customer's name.   1 2 3 4 5

3. Thank the customer by being genuinely enthusiastic.   1 2 3 4 5

4. Engage in small talk, if time allows.   1 2 3 4 5

5. Ask, "How may I help you?"   1 2 3 4 5

6. Be appropriately prompt.   1 2 3 4 5

7. Remember! Courtesy is the gold standard.   1 2 3 4 5

CONTINUED

CONTINUED

5 = Very frequently   4 = Frequently   3 = Neither frequently nor infrequently
2 = Infrequently   1 = Very infrequently

Meeting the Need

1. Listen (really!).   1 2 3 4 5

2. Ask questions to clarify.   1 2 3 4 5

3. Restate needs for understanding.   1 2 3 4 5

4. Offer options.   1 2 3 4 5

5. Explain all necessary information.   1 2 3 4 5

6. Reassure the customer.   1 2 3 4 5

7. Take action.   1 2 3 4 5

Follow-Through

1. Say "thank you" every time.   1 2 3 4 5

2. Do what you say you'll do—plus!   1 2 3 4 5

3. Send notes or letters or emails of appreciation.   1 2 3 4 5

4. Add a personal comment of appreciation.   1 2 3 4 5

5. Return calls and emails promptly.   1 2 3 4 5

6. Under-promise; over-deliver.   1 2 3 4 5

7. Ask to be of further service.   1 2 3 4 5

CONTINUED

CONTINUED

5 = Very frequently   4 = Frequently   3 = Neither frequently nor infrequently
2 = Infrequently   1 = Very infrequently

Handling Problems

1. Deal with the person.   1 2 3 4 5

2. Deal with the problem.   1 2 3 4 5

3. If necessary, try the Lion, Fox, or St. Bernard approach.   1 2 3 4 5

4. If none of the above work, get help!   1 2 3 4 5

5. Remember, the customer is always the customer, even   1 2 3 4 5
   when he's wrong.

6. Go the extra mile with Moment of Magic IV.   1 2 3 4 5